J.M.W. TURNER

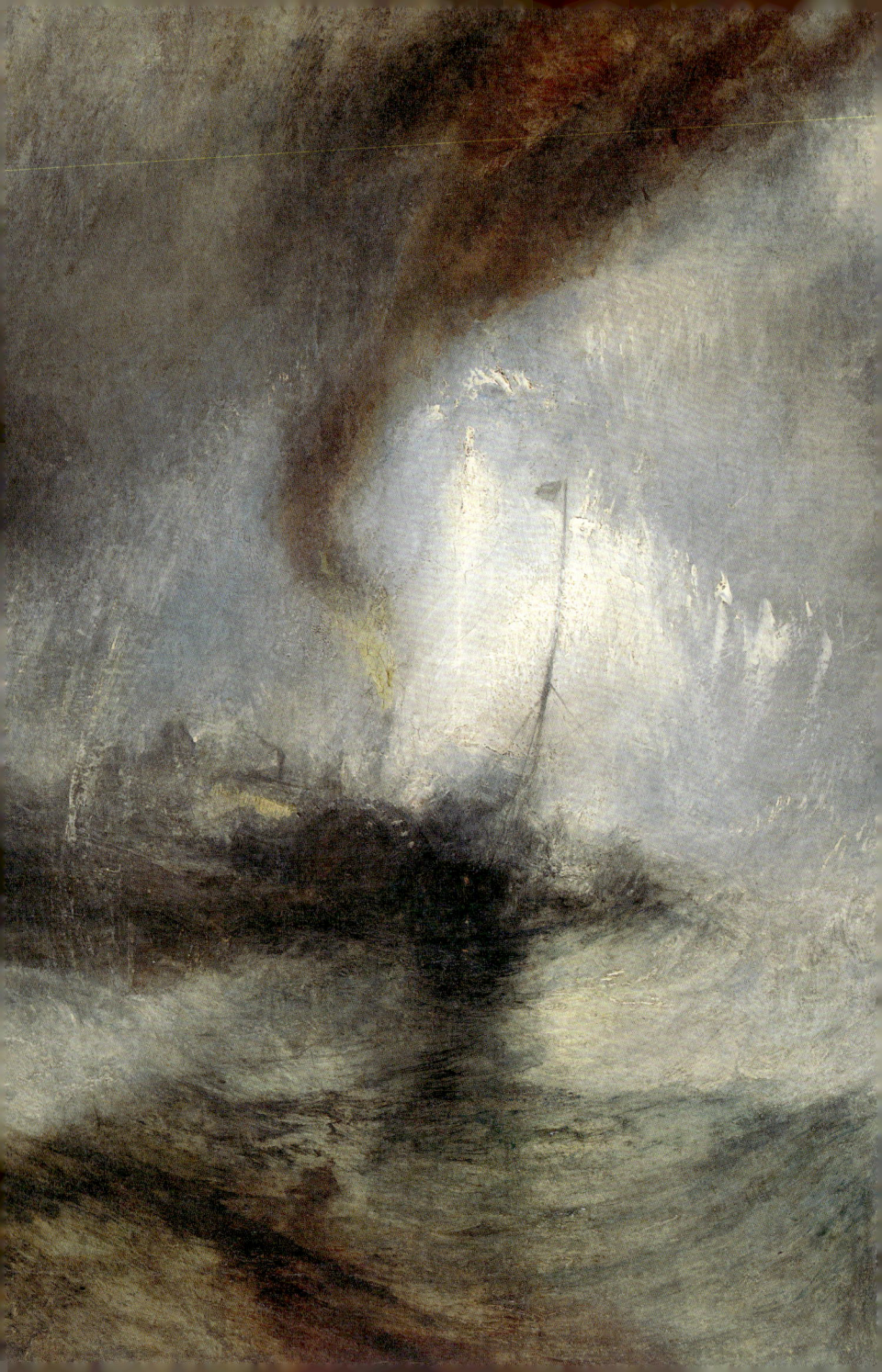

J.M.W. TURNER

ANDREW
LOUKES

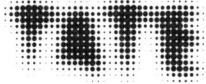

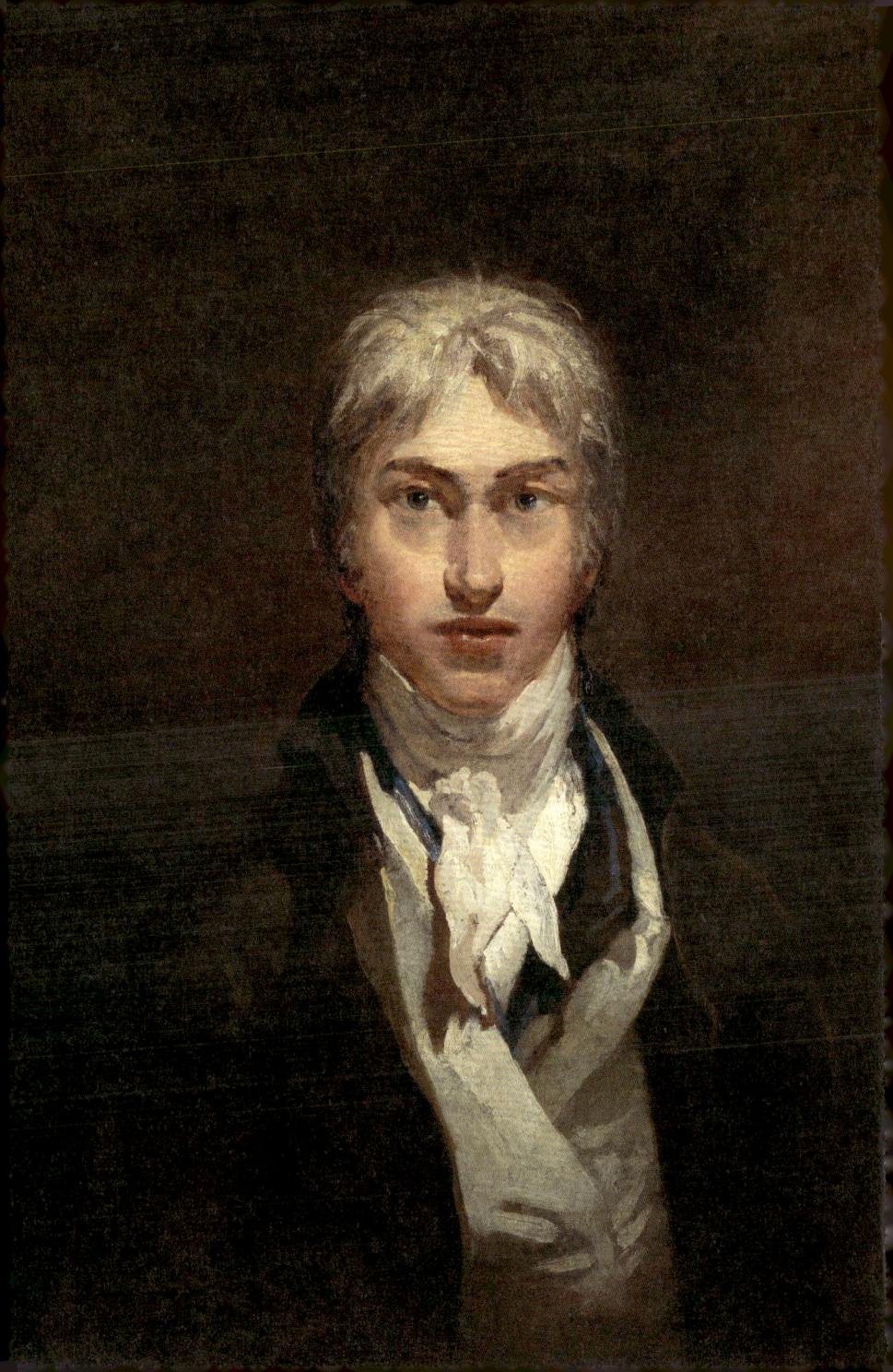

A WONDERFUL RANGE: THE RELEVANCE OF TURNER TODAY

Joseph Mallord William Turner (1775–1851) ranks alongside William Shakespeare, Jane Austen and Charles Dickens as a giant of British culture. Like these writers, he is among the historical figures represented on UK currency in recognition of their contribution to national achievement: the Bank of England twenty-pound note issued in 2020 reproduces both Turner's iconic self-portrait (opposite) and a detail from his most celebrated work, *The Fighting Temeraire* exh.1839 (pp.78–9). Turner is the first fine artist to have been accorded this honour.

Fifteen years earlier, when BBC Radio and the National Gallery put the 'Greatest Painting in Britain' to a public vote, *The Fighting Temeraire* won by a distance. At Tate, Turner's work forms around half of the collection and has been showcased in its own purpose-built gallery since 1987.[1] Three years before that, the Turner Prize – still awarded annually to a British contemporary artist – was named after the painter who had been 'innovative and controversial in his own day'.[2] And in 2011, the Turner Contemporary gallery at Margate opened, citing Turner's belief 'in the power of art as an agent for change'.[3] It is Turner whose works consistently set new records for historic British art sold at auction,[4] while the vast array of published literature about his life and work – not least that stemming from the dozens of exhibitions which have been devoted to him – greatly outweighs that relating to any other. In 2014, he was notably the subject of a feature film, Mike Leigh's critically acclaimed *Mr. Turner*.

The distinctive and familiar nature of Turner's art has merited the inclusion of the words 'Turneresque' and 'Turnerian' in English dictionaries, with the first recorded use of the latter coming as early as 1828.[5] Indeed, Turner's reputation and status were very much forged in his own time. Already an exhibiting artist with a growing client base during his teenage years, he was elected a full member of the Royal Academy (RA) – a prerequisite for any serious British artist of the period – in 1802, at the unprecedentedly early age of twenty-six. His subsequent official positions there included Professor of Perspective, while his virtuoso finishing touches to pictures at *Summer Exhibition* 'Varnishing Days' drew crowds of fellow exhibitors, who overwhelmingly held him in high regard.[6]

From early in his career Turner attracted the patronage of the aristocracy and landed gentry, and he completed a major royal commission in 1824 (p.20). The artist went

Self-portrait c.1798
Oil paint on canvas
74.3 × 58.4

on to find favour with the rising industrial and mercantile elite, and, through hundreds of published prints, his art also reached a far wider audience. Turner's plentiful sales and commissions enabled him to own several properties, including a large London townhouse with its own studio and gallery, and a self-designed Twickenham villa.[7] On his death, Turner's executors valued his estate at around £140,000 – some £16 million today – an accumulation of wealth unmatched by any other artist of his generation. Turner's packed funeral was held at St Paul's Cathedral, where his tomb is marked by a monumental marble statue.

Yet beyond the successes and accolades of his own lifetime and afterwards, Turner's lasting significance and popularity stems from the enduring power of his work. The artist's great contemporary John Constable perceptively recognised that Turner had 'a wonderful range of mind'.[8] This characteristic underpins an art which combines breathtaking technical advances – in both watercolours and oils, ranging in scale from miniature to massive – with evocations of infinite natural phenomena, myriad historical and literary narratives, and an equally wide-reaching engagement with his own age. Ultimately, Turner's explorations of shared human experience across these themes are timeless. That his sometimes challenging work can also be simultaneously profound and accessible – like that of Shakespeare, Austen and Dickens – only adds to its continued relevance and appeal.

STRONG INDICATIONS OF A FIRST-RATE ABILITY: BACKGROUND, TRAINING & BREAKTHROUGH

Superficially, Turner's extraordinary success is made more notable by his modest background, but actually this provided a perfect storm. He was born in Covent Garden, London, where his Devonian father was a barber and wig-maker; his mother's family had been London butchers for generations. Turner was possessed of a prodigious natural talent for drawing, and his youthful works were proudly displayed in the family salon by his always supportive father. This central London venue, a short distance from the RA's new home at Somerset House, ensured informed exposure to his earliest pictures. Meanwhile, the entrepreneurial environment of the artist's childhood resurfaced in his own approach to selling work for the rest of his life.

Turner's formative years were also marked by tragedy and disruption. The death of his four-year-old sister in 1783

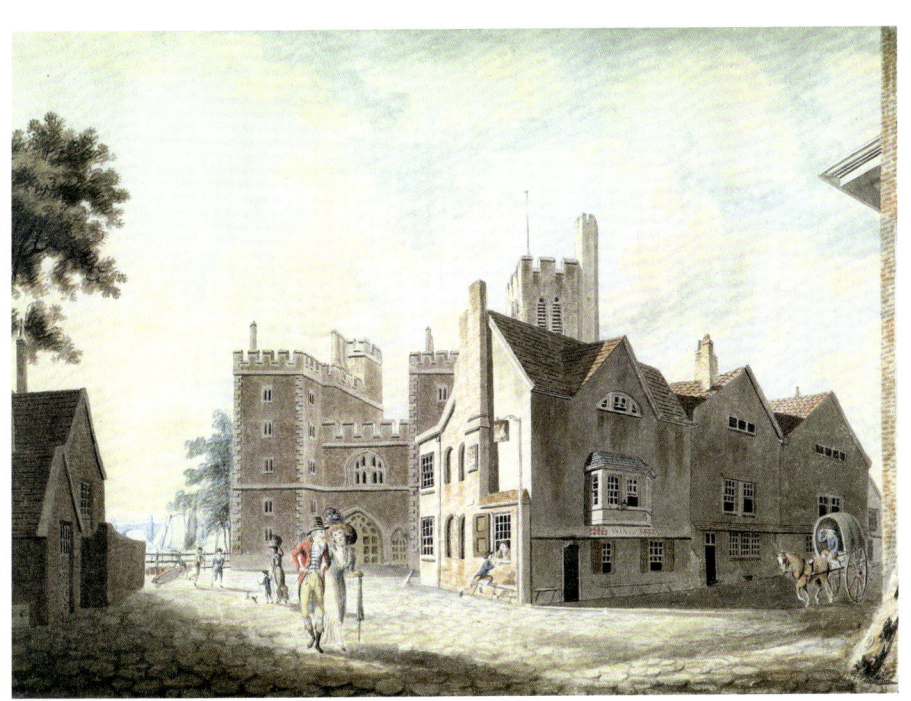

The Archbishop's Palace,
Lambeth c.1790
Watercolour on paper
26.7 × 38.1

exacerbated the declining mental health of Turner's mother, who would later be moved permanently to Bethlem Hospital. Perhaps in an attempt to find healthier surroundings for the only surviving child, young Turner – always known as William – was temporarily sent in 1785 to his kindly maternal uncle at Brentford, then a Middlesex town. Here, he was able to explore the western Thames – an area of lasting significance – and was employed to colour prints of British landscape scenery for a family friend.[9] Around the same time, aged twelve, he made a series of his own watercolours, possibly also based on prints by other artists (p.26).

In 1788, Turner was moved to Margate on the Kent coast, to live with members of the generous Trimmer family whom he had befriended in Brentford. Margate offered Turner his first experience of the sea, and the town was to become one of the artist's most special places. He attended schools both here and at Brentford, and as an outsider from London developed the independence and resilience which became defining features of his character.

Later in 1788, Turner returned to Covent Garden and

7

embarked on a range of local training and employment opportunities. Once more he coloured prints, but now at the fashionable London shop of the engraver John Raphael Smith. Additionally, he entered the offices of the architects William Porden and Thomas Hardwick, initially adding background skies and landscapes to their designs before graduating to fully realised drawings. Simultaneously, he took lessons with the watercolourist Thomas Malton Junior, whom Turner would later describe as 'my real master' and from whom he learned compositional techniques such as adopting low viewpoints.

Bolstered by the support and teaching of such well connected mentors, Turner was able to get through the highly competitive entry process for the RA's free school, then the only real formal education for aspiring British artists.[10] Once enrolled aged fourteen, he excelled at drawing sculptures and plaster casts in the Academy of the Antique (p.30) before progressing to the Academy of Living Models in 1792. Two years earlier, Turner had also announced himself as an exhibitor at the *Summer Exhibition* with a view of Lambeth Palace which demonstrated his ability to represent awkward architectural perspective (p.7). His reportage of the aftermath of a fire on London's Oxford Street (p.28), shown in 1792, carries Malton's lessons further, and by 1794 his standout talent was noted for the first time. One critic described his exhibits, including a view of Tintern Abbey – for which Turner had carefully made a preliminary version (p.31) – as 'among the best in the exhibition' and 'strong indications of a first-rate ability'.[11] These early offerings would be among the first of 259 RA exhibits during the course of Turner's long career.

A MORE ESSENTIAL TRUTH: TOURS & TRANSFORMATION

Turner's newfound ability to win praise was largely rooted in having experienced for himself the places he depicted. The artist had made in situ studies of Tintern Abbey, for example, during a tour of the English Midlands and South Wales in 1792. He undertook around forty such working excursions across Britain and Europe over his career, using some 300 sketchbooks and many hundreds of loose sheets of paper, which informed finished works that were usually completed in London. The opportunities afforded by such tours, both to gather visual reference material and to react

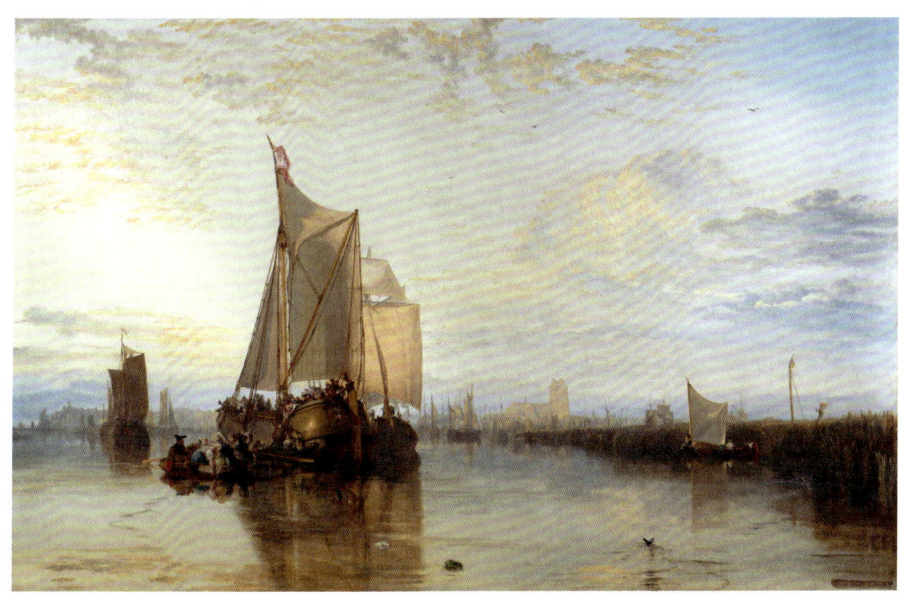

emotionally to subjects at first hand, became fundamental to his art. The artist's later supporter John Ruskin explained how Turner had reached 'by intuition and intensity of gaze a more essential truth than is seen at the surface of things'.[12]

Turner's first touring activity came in 1791 when he stayed with family friends, the Narraways, near Bristol. From here, he explored and sketched local sites and produced several finished watercolours, including a view of Malmesbury Abbey for which he clambered up into the ruins, inverting his teacher Malton's preference for a low viewpoint by exploring the dizzying effect of a higher one (p.27). In such compositions Turner began both to introduce vicarious excitement into his work and to improve on tradition – goals which continued throughout the rest of his career and were developed further through imaginary subjects based on the light-filled theatrical paintings of the French Royal Academician Philip James de Loutherbourg (p.29).

Additional inspiration came between 1794 and 1798 when Turner joined those young artists employed by the physician and amateur watercolourist Dr Thomas Monro to copy works in his collection by great pioneers of the medium. These included numerous examples by John Robert Cozens which Turner replicated in partnership with his friend Thomas Girtin, who largely did the pencilwork while Turner added washes

Dort, or Dordrecht, the Dort Packet-Boat from Rotterdam Becalmed exh.1818
Oil paint on canvas
157.5 × 233.7

of colour (p.32). Executing these so-called 'Monro School' works increased Turner's understanding of the expressive potential of watercolour while also introducing him to Italian and Swiss scenery.

During a temporary halt in the French Revolutionary Wars in 1802, Turner made the first of his twenty European journeys, travelling to the French and Swiss Alps via Paris, where he visited the Louvre and filled a sketchbook with annotated copies of old master paintings.[13] The mountainous landscapes he had seen in the watercolours of Cozens, however, were his ultimate goal, and for these he reserved the largest of the eight sketchbooks he took on the tour, capturing his most awe-inspiring views to date (p.43). Turner's second journey into Europe in 1817 took him across Belgium and back through Holland, where at Dordrecht, for example, he made numerous sketches. These would provide many of the details found in one of his most serene and feted works (p.9), a homage to the seventeenth-century Dutch marine painter Aelbert Cuyp.

Among the clearest examples of powerful imagery based on authentic experience is a watercolour of a coaching accident on the Mont Cenis Pass in 1820 (p.11), which saw the artist and his fellow passengers having to make their escape in blizzard conditions. Earlier on this third European excursion, Turner's principal destinations had been Venice, Naples and Rome, each of which he recorded in a group of freely handled watercolour studies (p.60). Inspired by Italian light, these demonstrated a new intensity of brightness and colour in his work, while the first exhibited painting derived from this tour (pp.60–1) combines this with both a tribute to another revered painter, Raphael, and a continued willingness to tackle challenging architectural perspectives.

THE SOIL IS BRITISH: ELEVATING THE NATIVE LANDSCAPE

Turner's interest in earlier artists was rooted in his student days at the RA, whose mission was to raise the status of British contemporary art by encouraging its members, students and exhibitors to inject their work with grand thematic purpose based on the example of the great European old masters. Turner is even likely to have heard the RA's founding president, Sir Joshua Reynolds, imparting these principles at the last of his famous 'Discourses' in 1790.

In his own inaugural lectures as Professor of Perspective in 1811 – ostensibly an illustrated course expanding on the lessons

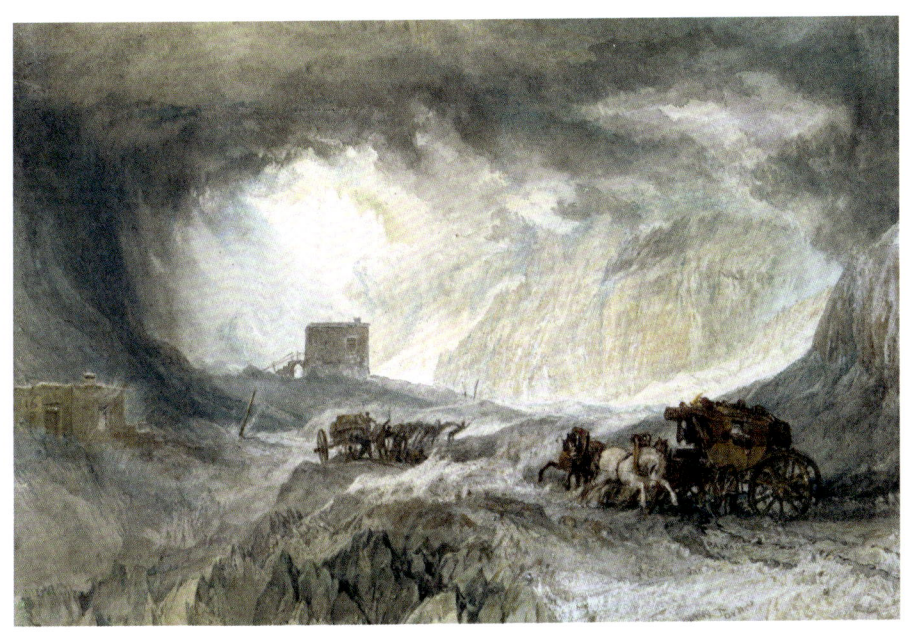

Passage of Mont Cenis 1820
Watercolour on paper
29.2 × 40

of architectural draughtsmanship – Turner echoed the vital importance of learning from the past, but also made a special point of encouraging his audience to pursue British subject matter. While the native landscape had been recorded in topographical prints and drawings for generations, it was not considered serious enough for the higher realms of art. Turner addressed this by making the point that 'the soil is British, so should be the harvest' and arguing that the 'endless variety' of native scenery was deserving of more inspiring treatment.[14]

Turner himself, of course, had already been keenly redefining the depiction of British subjects as a developing artist. Having first seen a painting by the Dutch master Rembrandt in 1795,[15] for example, he transposed something of its moonlight and firelight effects to a British cottage interior in a watercolour exhibited in 1796 (p.33). Yet to attain real acclaim it was necessary to produce work on a larger scale and in oil paint. No formal training in this medium was available at the RA, but the influence (and perhaps direct tutelage) of De Loutherbourg is evident in Turner's first exhibited painting (pp.34–5). Shown with the cottage interior, it likewise demonstrates the dramatic contrasts of Rembrandt's work, while also incorporating the Isle of Wight

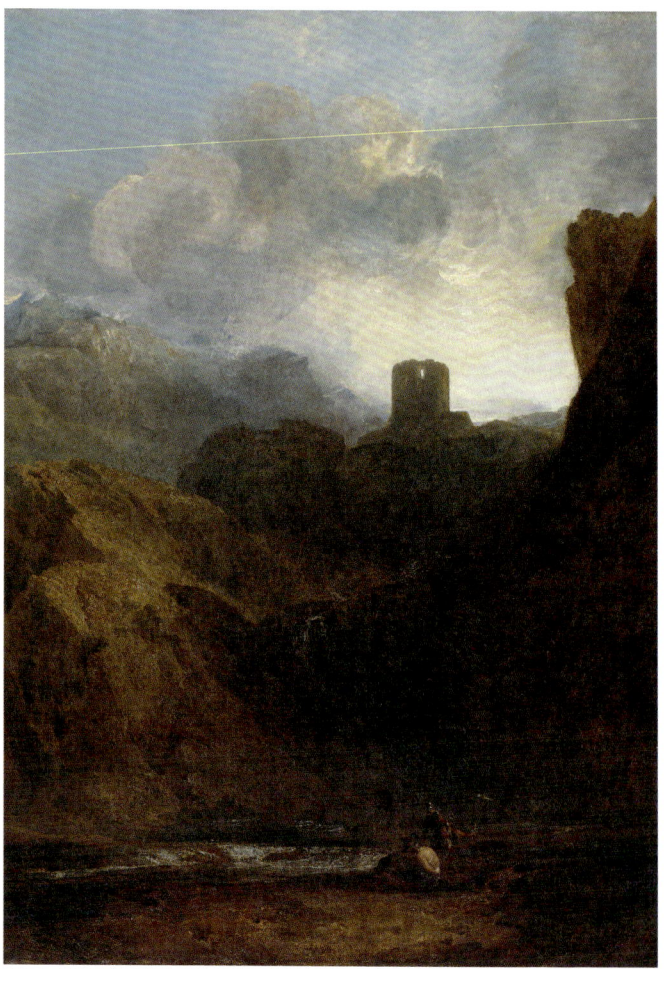

Dolbadarn Castle, North Wales
exh.1800
Oil paint on canvas
119.4 × 90.2

coastline which Turner had seen on a tour of the previous year. The imminent darkness which will soon impact the already dangerous work of night-time coastal fishing – the clouds have parted only momentarily – adds to the thrill of the work.

In its exciting evocation of danger, *Fishermen at Sea* demonstrates that Turner had also digested the fashionable aesthetic notion of the 'sublime'. His pursuit of yet more awesome subject matter, in the shape of native mountain scenery, led him to tour the Lake District (1797), North Wales (1799) and Scotland (1801), making extensive sketches and studies related to each of these excursions. The impact of the artist's resulting exhibits at the RA was deepened by his introduction of poetic quotations in the accompanying printed catalogues (p.37). His exhibited Welsh subjects of 1800 additionally reference disturbing historical contexts – the thirteenth-century expulsion of the Welsh bards by the English (pp.40–1) and the contemporary confinement of Owain Goch by his brother in Dolbadarn Castle (p.12) – and in each work the immensity of nature dwarfs the narrative's small human figures.

The success of such exhibits led to Turner's election as an Associate of the Royal Academy in 1799 and a full member in 1802. By 1805, the then thirty-year-old artist had taken his own tenancy of a West London address on Harley Street, to which he added his own gallery as a secondary shop window. In the same year he also rented a Thames-side cottage at Isleworth, exploring the Thames by boat and indulging in the growing trend among British artists for making coloured sketches outdoors (p.76). These informed a subsequent series of works in which Turner elevates the river into an Arcadian paradise (p.14). Within this landscape he acquired a patch of land in Twickenham in 1807 on which to build a villa for use as a retreat. In one idealised representation of the countryside west of London, exhibited in 1809, he additionally demonstrated a growing willingness to engage with current social developments, highlighting the latest trend in intensive farming (p.50).

Such agricultural matters were of particular interest to one of Turner's greatest patrons, George O'Brien Wyndham, Third Earl of Egremont, whose seat at Petworth House in West Sussex the artist visited in the same year to make sketches for a commissioned painting (p.51). For some years, the provision of such country house views had been another of his central lines of work, and his patron's receptiveness to contemporary artists ensured that Petworth would remain a place of continued importance to Turner for years to come: Egremont bought and commissioned twenty of his oil paintings, and the artist made some 150 evocative watercolour sketches there during a stay of 1827.

A visit to another of Turner's great supporters, Sir Walter Fawkes of Farnley Hall, in Yorkshire, prompted a winter scene exhibited in 1813 (p.55) which appears to include the elder of Turner's two illegitimate daughters by Sarah Danby, the

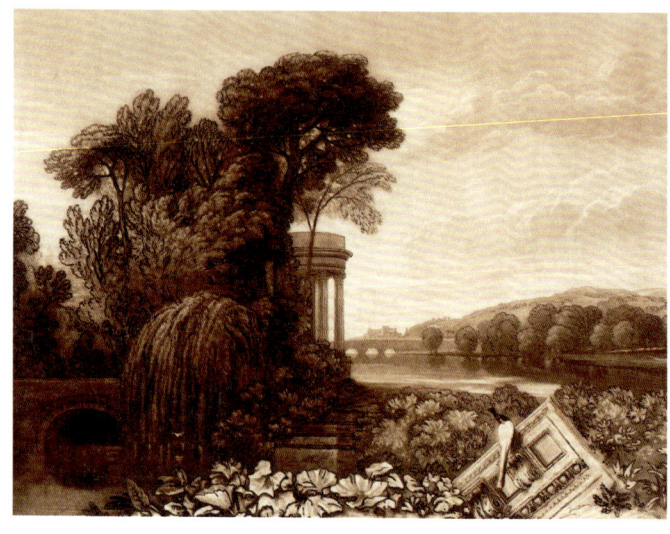

Isis – Picture in the Possession of the Earl of Egremont, etched by Turner and engraved by William Say, published 1819
Etching and mezzotint on paper 26 × 26.1

widowed aunt of his housekeeper Hannah. The same girl also features to the left in his view of the Tamar Valley, based on sketches made during a tour of Devon in 1813 and exhibited in 1815 (p.56).[16] This painting is among many grounded in the visual language of Turner's greatest source of artistic inspiration, the seventeenth-century French landscape painter Claude Lorrain. Turner's English Arcadia, however, is here contemporised by the inclusion of distant mining activity.

AFTER TURNER: THE CENTRAL ROLE OF PRINTMAKING IN TURNER'S ART

The provision of watercolours for reproduction by professional printmakers was a major dimension of Turner's work, both creatively and financially, for most of his career. Over 700 such prints featured in numerous publications during his lifetime, beginning in the mid-1790s with straightforward topographical compositions. Between 1807 and 1819 Turner published his own more ambitious series, the *Liber Studiorum*, with the outlines etched by himself. The seventy-one subjects, divided into different categories of landscape, were intended to illustrate the range of his art and included new and existing compositions (above).

The forty designs Turner contributed to *Picturesque Views of the Southern Coast of England*, published between 1814 and 1826, also move beyond mere landscape records and instead offer more vital representations of time and place. His dynamic view of Brighton (p.15), for example, not only showcases two brand-new constructions – the Chain Pier and the Royal Pavilion – but also contrasts modern tourism with the perilous work of local fishermen. His watercolour of St Mawes, Cornwall was preceded by an oil of the same subject, both of which record a surplus of pilchards on the shore, reflecting one outcome of restricted international trade during the Napoleonic Wars (p.54). For *Views in Sussex*, published in 1819, the ecological impact of the county's iron trade is alluded to in his view of the Vale of Ashburnham (p.16), where trees are felled to make charcoal for smelting.

Turner's skill in compressing layers of observation and commentary into the small scale required for prints developed further in the 1820s. His representation of Newcastle-upon-Tyne for *The Rivers of England*, for example, combines the city's burgeoning architectural skyline and range of shipping with growing atmospheric pollution from its metalworks, collieries and lime-kilns (p.62). A later view of Northampton (p.70) is largely a celebration of the re-election of the county's MP, Lord Althorp, who became a central figure in bringing about the sweeping changes to the electoral system made by the Reform Act of 1832. This watercolour was among those made by Turner for *Picturesque Views in England and Wales*, which eventually included ninety-six of his designs between 1827 and 1837. The view of Northampton, however, was possibly considered too politically charged for publication and, like that of the Houses of Parliament ablaze in the fire of 1834 (p.71), was among those never engraved.

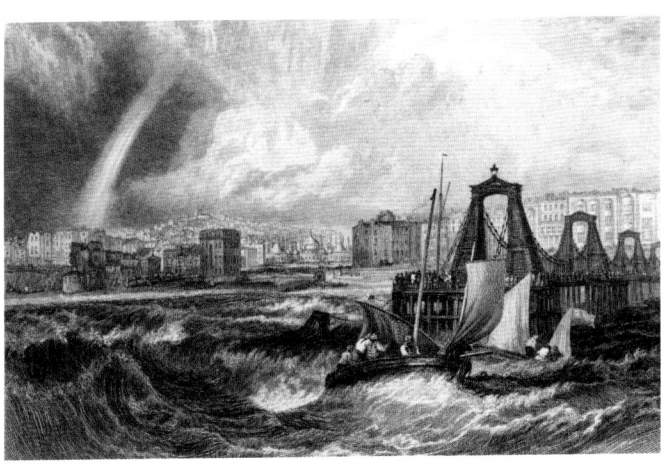

Brighthelmston, Sussex,
engraved by George Cooke,
published 1825
Engraving on paper
15.4 × 23.1

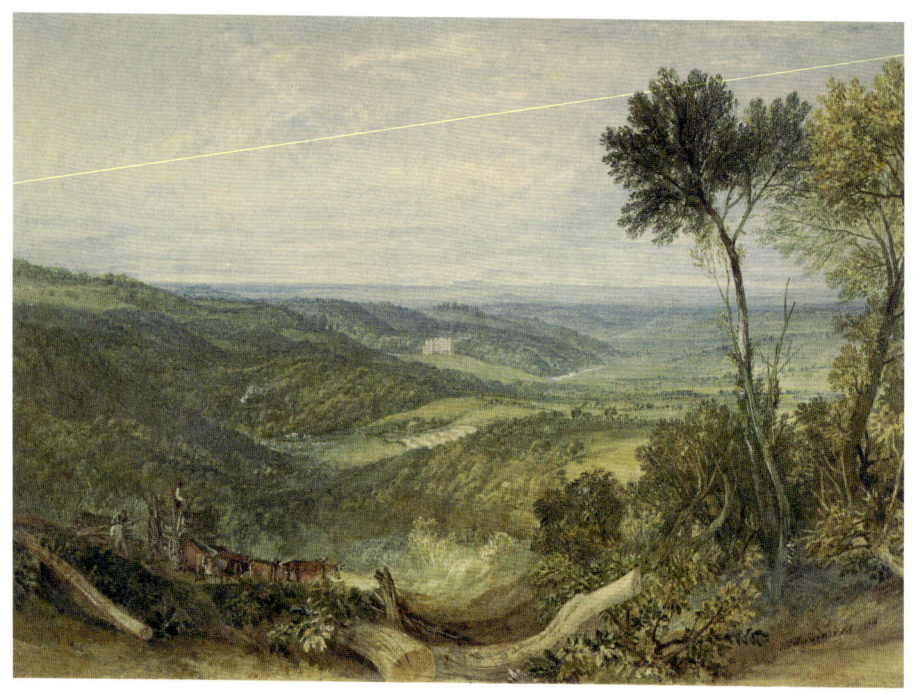

In the early 1830s Turner was commissioned to provide imagery for a new venture entitled *Turner's Annual Tour*. Twenty-one views of the River Loire were published in 1833, followed by successive volumes charting the Seine in 1834 and 1835. These groups represented a fresh departure in comprising complete sequences of prints, issued together rather than serially, and devoted to his designs alone. For his watercolours of the Loire the artist utilised a group of sketches made during a tour of northern France in 1826, including a number on small sheets of blue paper (p.63), which became the format for all the finished designs (p.17). These publications proved highly popular, excelling in their distillation of expansive landscape scenery and complex architectural topography.

During the same period, Turner worked in an even more reduced format for editions of poetry by writers including Lord Byron and Samuel Rogers (p.69), the former having also influenced several works on a larger scale. Turner additionally enjoyed a particularly fruitful relationship with Sir Walter Scott, including a view of his eventual burial place for the *Poetical Works* (pp.68–9).

The Vale of Ashburnham 1816
Watercolour on paper
38 × 56.4

Rouen Cathedral c.1832
Gouache and watercolour
on blue paper
14 × 19.4

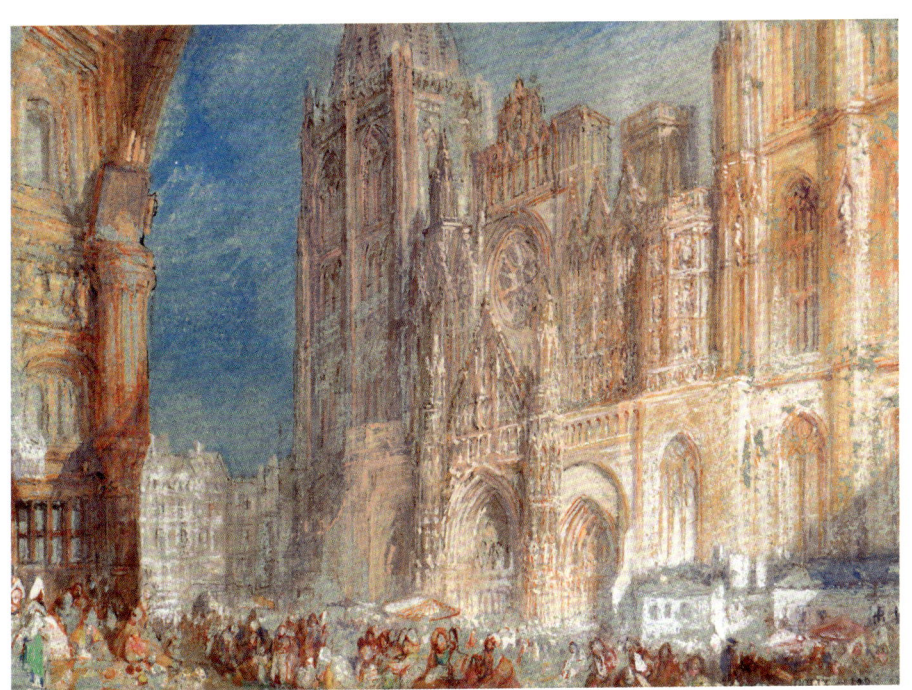

COLOSSAL POWER: REINVENTING MARINE & HISTORY PAINTING

While Turner won his earliest notice for watercolours of architectural landscapes, it was as a painter of the sea that his name was made, and he remained best known as a marine artist throughout his life. His first exhibited oil painting had been a well-received sea-piece (pp.34–5), and this was followed in the early 1800s by a succession of increasingly striking nautical compositions. His painting of Calais Pier, exhibited in 1803 (p.44), was later described by Ruskin as the first demonstration of 'Turner's colossal power'.[17] This somewhat jingoistic picture evokes the artist's experience of landing in France for his tour of 1802, showing the British ferry attempting to reach its mooring in rough sea amid incompetent local fisherfolk.

A still more perilous scene was the imagined shipwreck which Turner exhibited at his own gallery in 1805 (p.45). Having been initially sold to another of the artist's great patrons, Sir John Fleming Leicester, the work was soon reacquired by Turner and its engraved reproduction proved very lucrative. The painting possibly draws on both the popular 1804 edition of William Falconer's poem *The Shipwreck* (first published in 1762) and the real dangers of sea travel which were all too familiar for an early nineteenth-century audience: a terrible disaster off the coast of Weymouth in 1805, for example, ended in great losses, including that of the ship's captain, John Wordsworth, brother to the famous poet.

Later in his career, Turner claimed how an early sighting of a print based on a painting by the seventeenth-century Dutch marine painter William van de Velde had 'made me a painter'.[18] More generally, through his understanding of this strand of Netherlandish art – also admired in the work of Cuyp, Jacob van Ruisdael, Jan van Goyen and others – Turner was able to develop his own approach to the genre. Occasionally, he combined these influences with overtly Dutch subject matter: a painting exhibited in 1819 shows a vessel stranded at the entrance to the River Maas which has shed its cargo of oranges, symbolising the losses felt by the royal House of Orange during the Napoleonic Wars (p.59). Another, shown in 1832, takes the more historical theme of the arrival from Holland of William III following the Glorious Revolution of 1688 (p.72).

If Turner excelled at sea-painting, he also realised that the successful representation of historical or literary subjects – particularly those depicting classical mythology – would see him held in highest esteem. An early attempt at so-called 'history painting' illustrates the poet Virgil's account of the Trojan warrior Aeneas negotiating his entrance to the Underworld (p.36). A few years later, another composition depicted the mischievous removal of the golden apple by Eris, the Greek goddess of discord, which would lead to the Trojan War (p.48). Turner's debt in this picture to another highly regarded seventeenth-century French painter, Nicolas Poussin, was particularly praised.[19]

For his representation of the ancient Carthaginian general Hannibal crossing the Alps to invade Italy, Turner set the scene within a landscape inspired by one of his visits to Yorkshire (pp.52–3). The military leader, mounted on an elephant, is shown as a distant figure, while his rearguard is slaughtered and looted by Swiss tribesmen. If its exhibition in 1812 might have been intended to evoke the flawed advancement of Napoleon, it was Turner's combination of natural and narrative sublime qualities which impressed the reviewers.

The ultimate decline of the Carthaginian Empire was treated by Turner five years later in a painting which illustrates how, in the sphere of history painting especially, it was Claude Lorrain who remained most influential to him (p.57). Turner's lengthy stay in Rome in 1828 prompted further Claude-inspired Italian subjects (p.66), which subsequently evolved into entirely unique and otherworldly treatments of classical narrative (pp.67, 74–5).

TAPPING THE FURNACE: WAR, TECHNOLOGY & ATROCITY

Towards the end of his career Turner repainted an interior scene he had begun decades earlier, transforming it into a celebration of the recent moment when the giant bronze statue of the Duke of Wellington, destined for Hyde Park Corner in London, was released from its mould (below).[20] Explaining in his accompanying RA catalogue entry that this process was called 'tapping the furnace', he fused into one image two defining themes of his lifetime: war and industry.

While the impact of war on the home front is referenced in many of Turner's British scenes, the fighting is also treated explicitly. Based on a drawing by an officer present, an early watercolour depicts the British assault in 1799 on Seringapatam, the stronghold of Napoleon's Indian ally, Tipu Sultan (pp.38–9). Subsequent pictures include a *Battle of Trafalgar* partially based on sketches made on board Lord Nelson's flagship the *Victory* following her return to Sheerness (p.49). Amid a forest of masts and the smoke of battle, Turner represents the fatal shooting of Nelson by a French sniper.

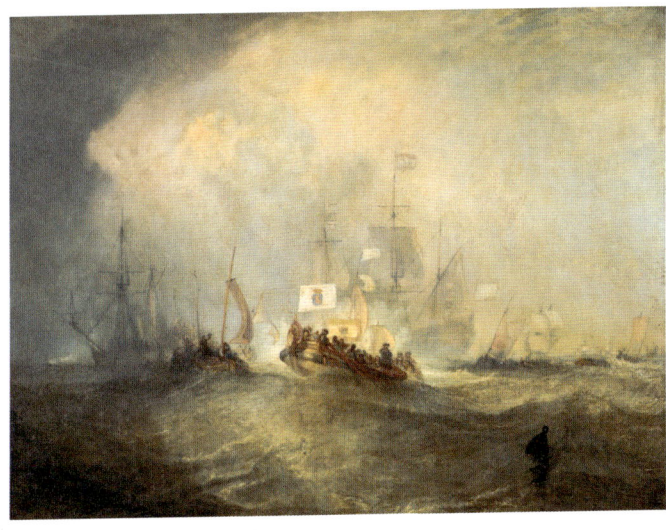

The Hero of a Hundred Fights
c.1800–10, reworked and exh.1847
Oil paint on canvas
90.8 × 121.3

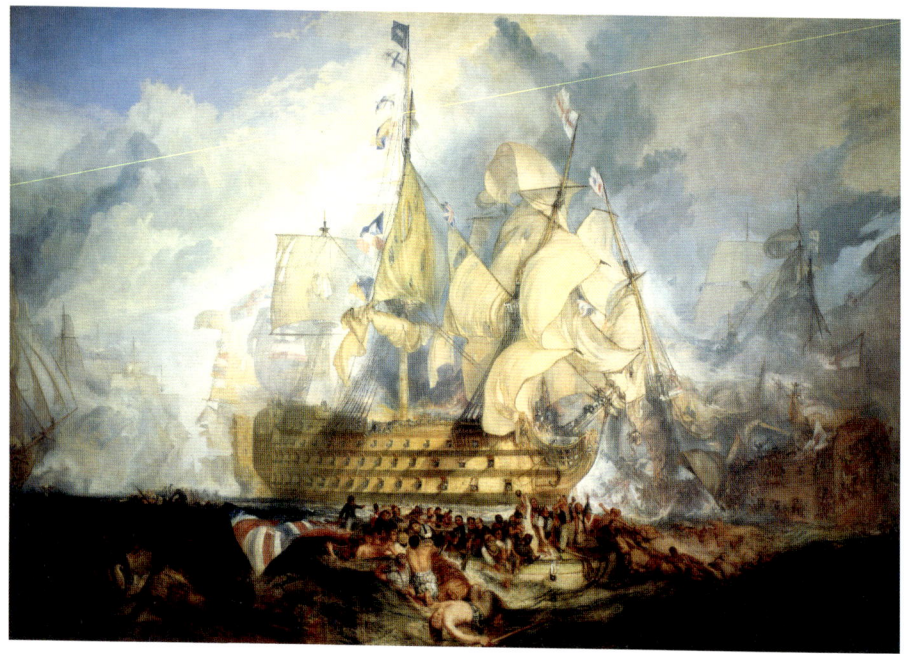

Several years later, his largest painting was another depiction of the Battle, commissioned by George IV around 1822 and the only one of his pictures to enter the royal collection, albeit briefly – it was given to the Greenwich Hospital in 1829 (above). Turner controversially conflated many of the known details of the event into one scene and placed the rescue of drowning sailors in the foreground.

Equally contentious was Turner's representation of the Battle of Waterloo in a painting shown in 1818 and done using sketches from his 1817 tour of the Low Countries (p.58). In this work, he also emphasised the suffering of the combatants, whose womenfolk grimly search for their bodies by torchlight. A distant flare signals the presence of looters, while to the right the British stronghold – the farmhouse at Hougoumont – still burns. Later in his career, Turner produced a series of paintings in related pairs, one of which contrasts the fate of Napoleon in exile with the serene burial at sea of the artist's friend and fellow painter David Wilkie from a steamboat off the coast of Gibraltar (pp.82, 83).

Three years earlier, in his iconic image of the *Temeraire*, Turner had made similar thematic connections between

The Battle of Trafalgar,
21 October 1805
1822–4
Oil paint on canvas
261.5 × 368.5

reminders of war and peaceful dignity (pp.78–9). Here, the former ship of the line which had been central to the British victory at Trafalgar is drawn by steam-tug up the Thames to her final berth. Turner emphasises the poignancy of the moment by showing the great vessel fully rigged rather than broken down to the hulk she had become by this point, and sets the scene against an impossible eastern sunset and a new moon rising to echo the end of one era and the beginning of another. While there is wistfulness in this narrative, many of the artist's own voyages had been made possible by steam travel and feature in works such as that inspired by his trip around the Scottish island of Staffa to see Fingal's Cave in 1831 (below).

Turner elaborated further on the dynamism of steam power in his famous painting of the *Ariel* caught in the eye of a storm and sending up distress signals (p.88). This picture challenged his audience, who variously described it as painted 'with his whole array of kitchen stuff' and 'soapsuds and whitewash'. The artist claimed, however, that he 'did not paint it to be understood' and that he had been aboard, lashed to the mast.[21] While this seems unlikely (there was no *Ariel* that sailed from Harwich), Turner was perhaps poetically evoking both the spirit of that name from Shakespeare's play *The Tempest* and the Greek hero Ulysses who was tied to his ship to avoid being lured by the deadly Sirens.

Two years later, Turner exhibited his only painting of

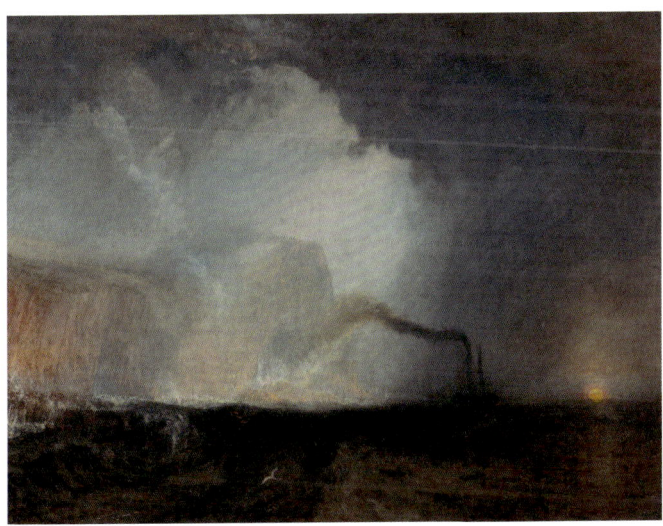

Staffa, Fingal's Cave exh.1832
Oil paint on canvas
90.8 × 121.3

a passenger train – a steam engine on the Great Western Railway, crossing the Thames using Isambard Kingdom Brunel's recently completed viaduct at Maidenhead (p.89). Again, he contrasts the new with the old: the speed of the train against that of the hare just ahead of it – the animal now almost faded away – and the line taken by the modern track through a bucolic landscape. Turner had pursued a similar theme in his earlier painting of the Chichester Canal, newly excavated through the West Sussex countryside, commissioned by Lord Egremont for Petworth House around 1828 (pp.64–5).

Other modern subjects were painted for patrons of a different class, who had made their fortunes through manufacturing. One such example was an elegiac representation for the Manchester cotton magnate Henry McConnel of coals being loaded onto ships at Newcastle by night (below), which both celebrates British industry and hints at the environmental impact it is already having. Some ten years later, the artist produced four scenes of whale-hunting for the London lamp-oil entrepreneur Elhanan Bicknell, whose product was dependent on the activity depicted. Despite having bought several of Turner's other works, however, he ultimately rejected the whaling pictures (p.90).

The artist also tackled yet grimmer aspects of modernity in his two last decades. An unfinished painting of the mid-1830s represents a disaster at sea which possibly reflects recent events: the wreck of a ship transporting female convicts in 1833

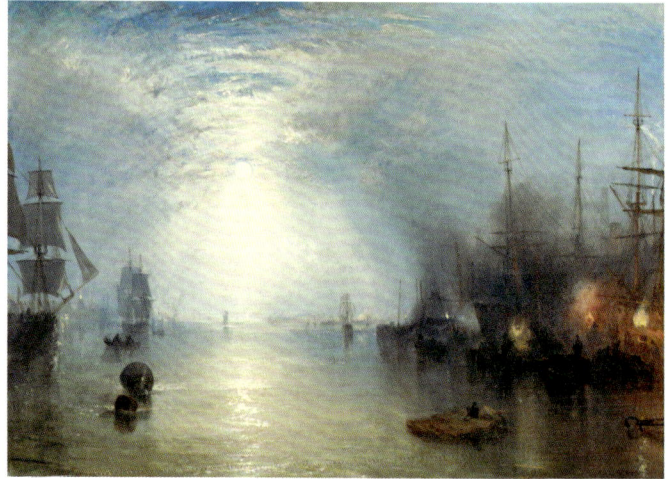

Keelmen Heaving in Coals by Moonlight exh.1835
Oil paint on canvas
92.3 × 122.8

Slavers Throwing Overboard the Dead and Dying, Typhon Coming On exh.1840
Oil paint on canvas
91 × 13.8

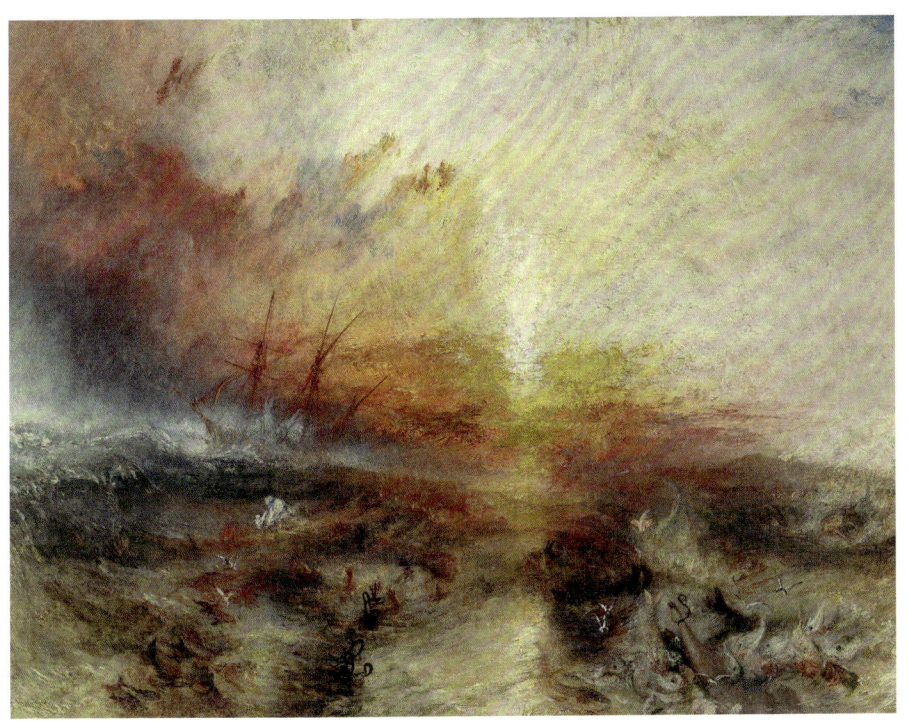

and/or the destruction by fire of another carrying emigrants in 1832, both resulting in catastrophic losses en route to Australia (p.73).[22] If Turner considered this subject too raw for public display, the exhibition of his hellish vision of terminally ill African captives being jettisoned into the sea in order for the ship's captain to claim insurance money was timed perfectly to coincide with the World Anti-Slavery Convention of 1840 in London (above). Alluding to a real atrocity of 1781,[23] Turner's politicised and humanitarian statement is perhaps tinged with the personal shame of having both invested, unsuccessfully, in a Jamaican estate thirty-five years earlier and benefited from the patronage of pro-slavery clients as a younger artist.[24] Turner had, however, subsequently formed far firmer connections with abolitionists, including Fawkes and Egremont, and in 1828 pointedly issued an engraving of his painting of the biblical Deluge (pp.46–7) – featuring a heroic black figure – with a dedication to the prominent anti-slavery campaigner John Joshua Proby, First Earl of Carysfort.[25]

THROUGH VAPOUR: LOOKING BACKWARDS & MOVING FORWARDS

When he exhibited *Sun rising through vapour; Fishermen cleaning and selling fish* (below) in 1807 Turner followed an approach he had established in the 1790s of introducing certain pictures in the context of the weather conditions or times of day they describe. This progressive emphasis on atmospheric effects became a defining preoccupation and inspired many subsequent generations of artists.[26] Yet Turner's art remained fundamentally rooted in the example of earlier painters: in reflection of its debt to the Netherlandish marine tradition, *Sun rising through vapour* was retitled *Dutch Boats* when re-exhibited at his own gallery. Moreover, Turner's ultimate bequest of this particular painting to the National Gallery stipulated it should hang alongside works by Claude, with whom he would therefore be forever connected.[27]

While the paintings of Turner's final decade reflect a heightened tendency towards vaporous effects, they too look backwards in revisiting earlier favourite locations and subjects. He repeatedly returned to Margate, for example, lodging with the widow Sophia Booth, with whom he would also spend his final years in Chelsea. A painting of the beach, exhibited in 1840, contains a juvenile narrative which possibly reflects childhood associations with the town (p.77). In an echo of *The Fighting Temeraire* of the previous year, the titular new moon rises above a steamboat – but here the onset of modernity has extra resonance within a landscape redolent with personal memories of a previous age. While the painting is equally

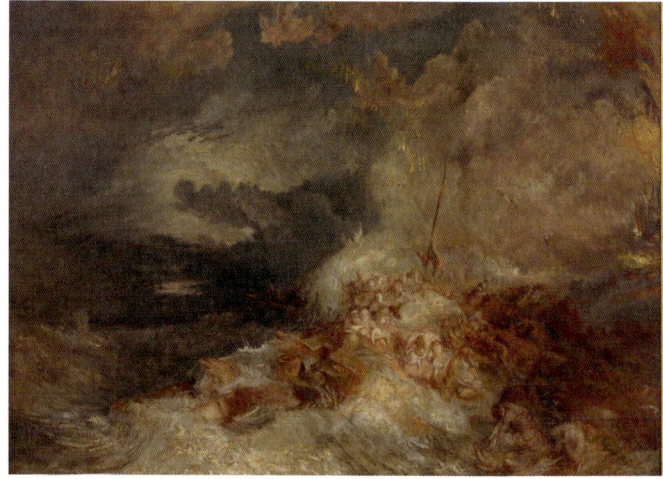

Sun rising through vapour: Fishermen cleaning and selling fish, before 1807
Oil paint on canvas
134 × 179.5

a celebration of natural phenomena, this interest was given its freest rein in dozens of studies, in watercolour and oil, of the sea (pp.84–5). Never intended for public display, these paintings have contributed greatly to Turner's popularity with modern audiences accustomed to impressionist and abstract art.

Turner also returned to Venice in 1840, making over a hundred watercolour studies (p.80) which informed a group of oil paintings on his return. With their straightforwardly descriptive titles and lack of narrative, these shimmering Venetian scenes proved highly sought-after; a view from the artist's hotel, for example, was bought by the horse-dealer Robert Vernon, whose major collection of British art was largely given to the nation in 1847 (p.81).

Turner continued to travel in Europe beyond his seventieth birthday, twice visiting the coast of northern France in 1845, preceded by annual trips to the Swiss Alps between 1841 and 1844. Following the commercial success of his Venetian paintings, Turner's later Swiss tours provided material for a series of watercolours marketed at existing middle-class clients. A view of the Rigi, near Lucerne (p.86), bought by Elhanan Bicknell, formed one of a series where the mountain became a focus for changing effects of light and colour, prefiguring groups of works based on a single motif by later artists from Paul Cezanne to Andy Warhol.

Although these watercolours are defined by Turner's bold use of colour, incorporating the latest manufactured pigments, this had long been a target for the critical mockery of his exhibited oil paintings.[28] The jibes became yet more prevalent in the 1840s and unfavourable comparisons with his earlier work were often made. In private, Turner revisited a period of more universal approval in a group of oil paintings based on his Liber Studiorum prints, reinvented in fluid colour (p.87). The artist's final exhibits in 1850 also looked backwards in marking a return to classical narrative (p.91). Featuring four episodes from Virgil's Aeneid, these paintings invest the most esteemed category of subject matter from the artist's youth with his vibrant technique of later years. In doing so they fittingly reflect a lifetime's devotion to the constant evolution of art.

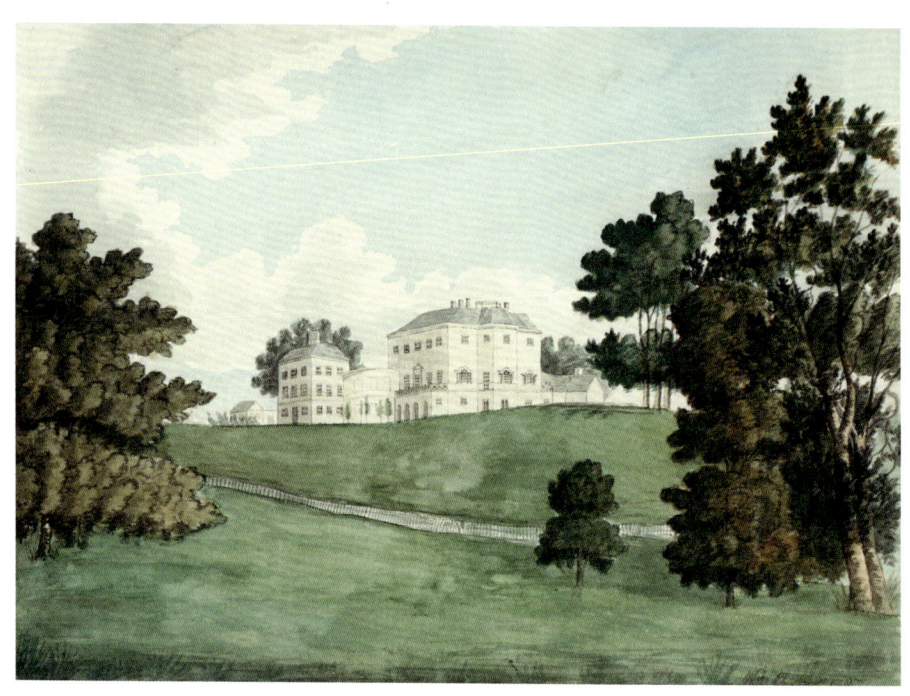

View of Nuneham House from
the Thames 1787
Watercolour and pencil
on paper
30.2 × 42.2

The West Tower of
Malmesbury Abbey 1791
Pencil, watercolour and
pen and brown ink on
paper
32.7 × 24.8

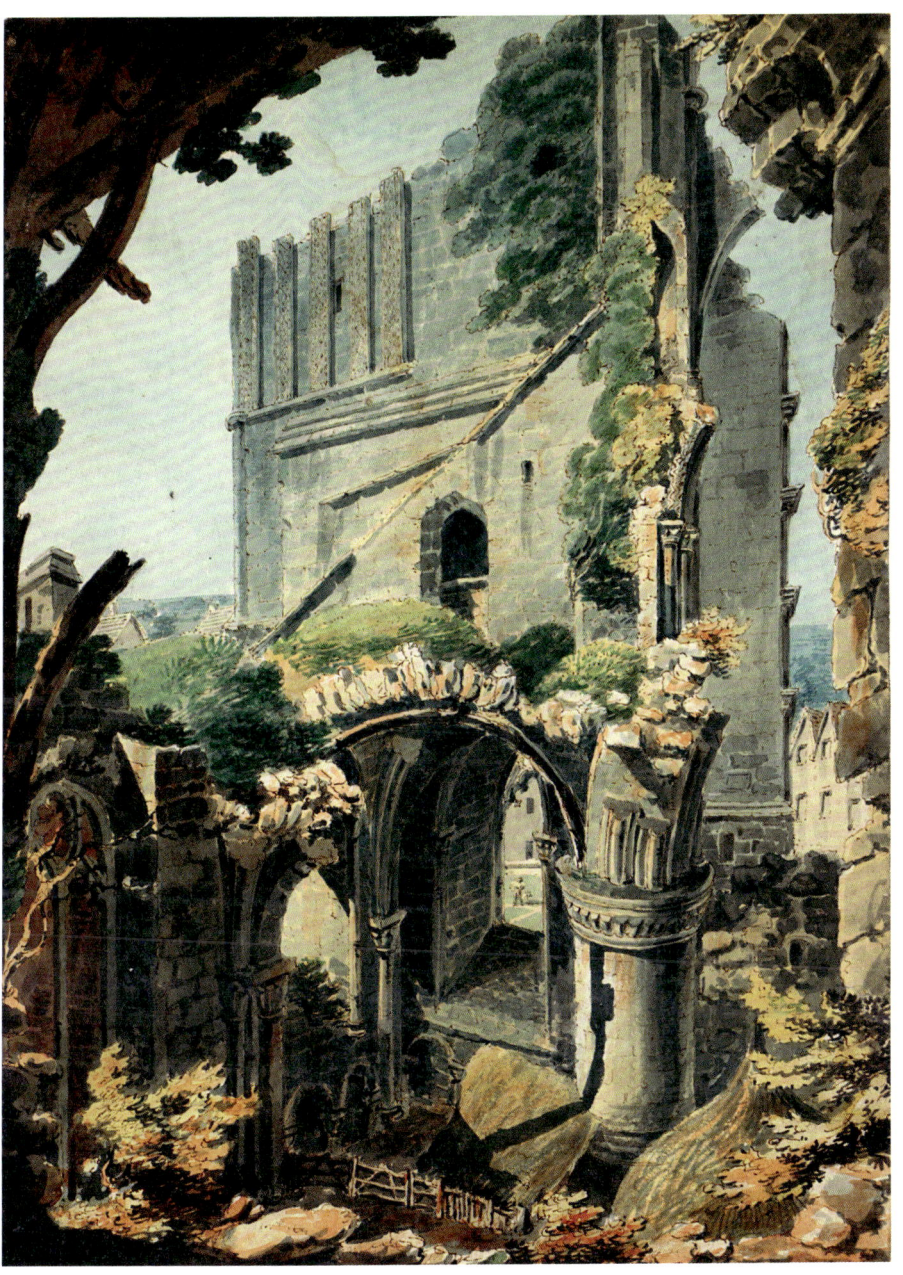

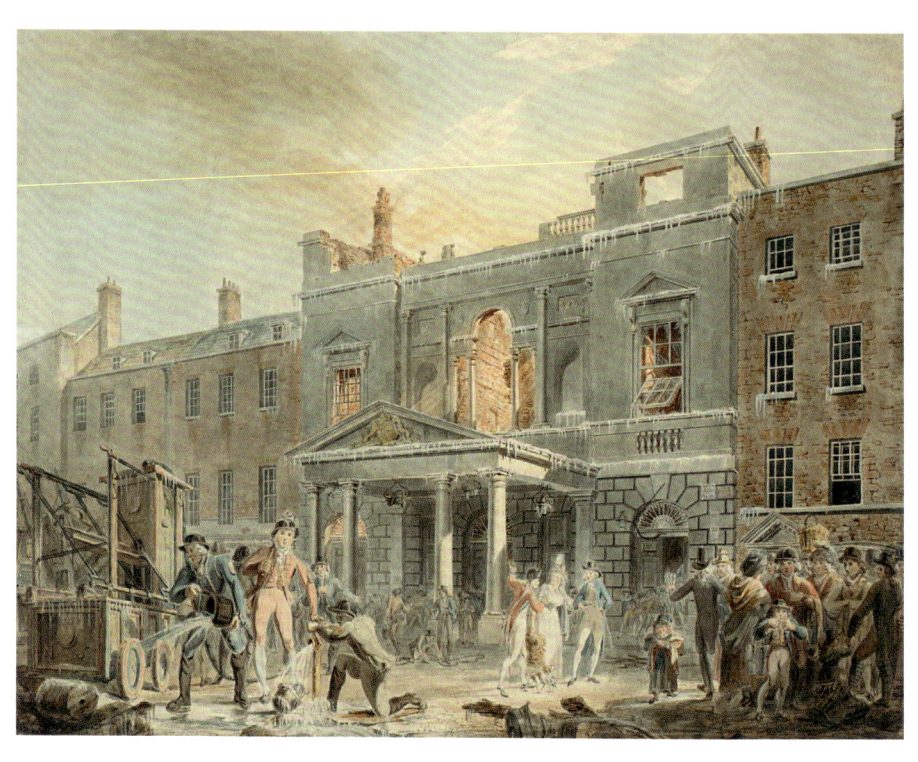

*The Pantheon, the Morning
after the Fire* exh.1792
Pencil, watercolour and
bodycolour on card
39.5 × 51.5

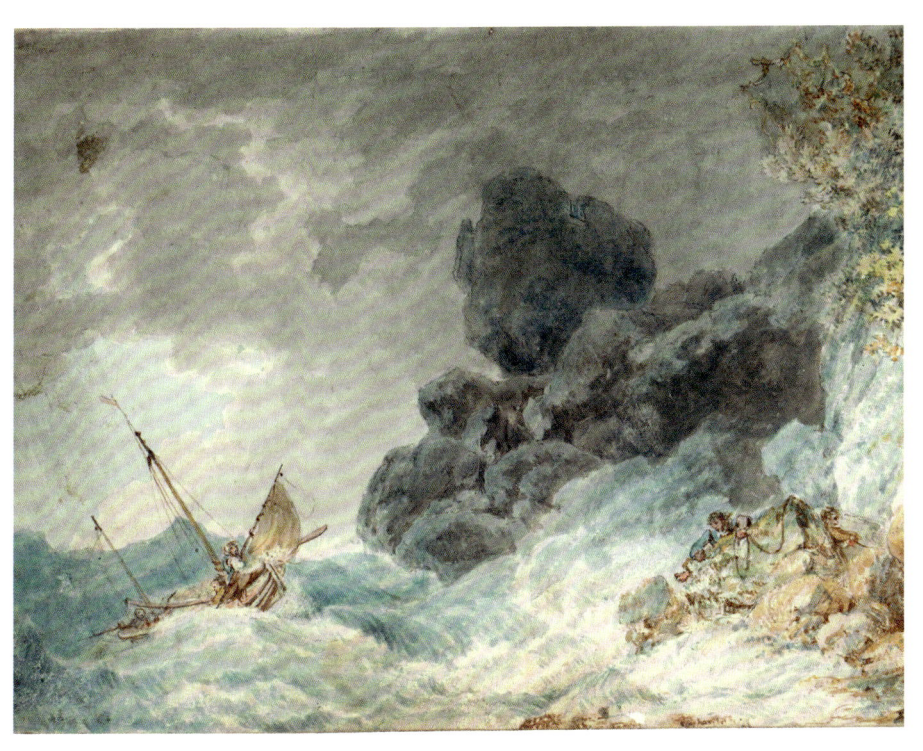

A Rocky Shore, with Men
Attempting to Rescue
a Storm-Tossed Boat 1792–3
Pencil and watercolour
on paper
16.1 × 23.2

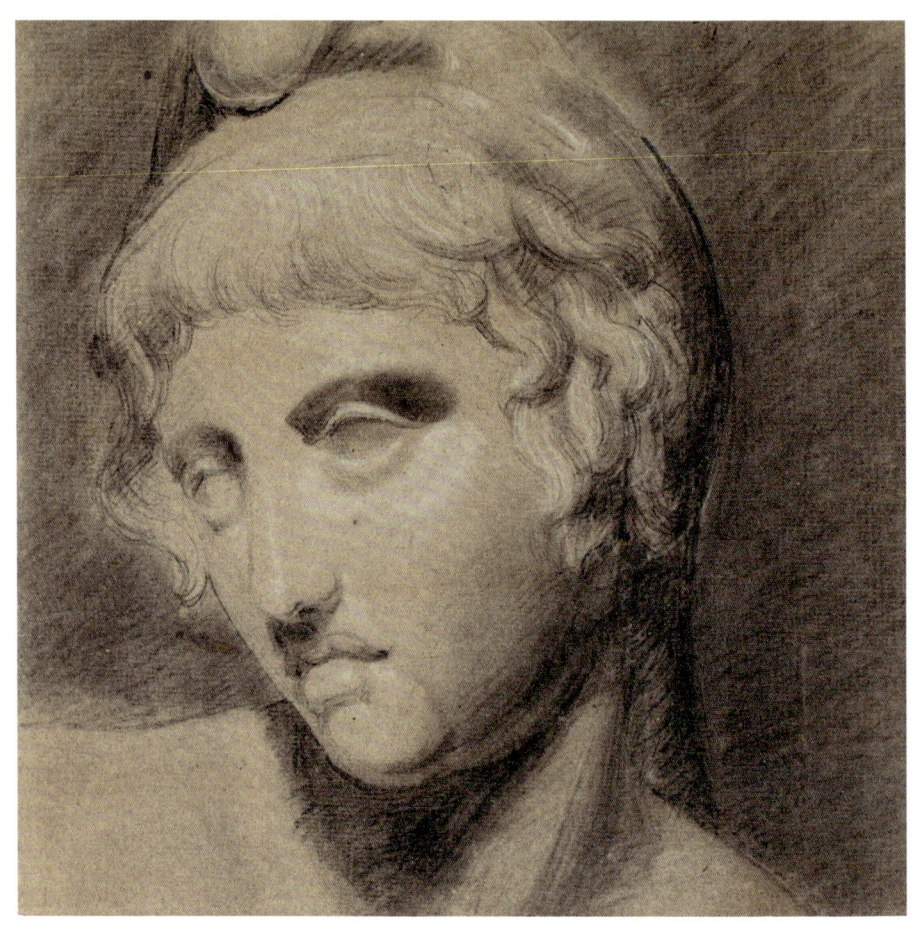

Study of the Head of Paris
?1792–3
Chalk on paper
27.5 × 27.1

Tintern Abbey: The Crossing
and Chancel, Looking towards
the East Window 1794
Pencil and watercolour
on paper
35.9 × 25

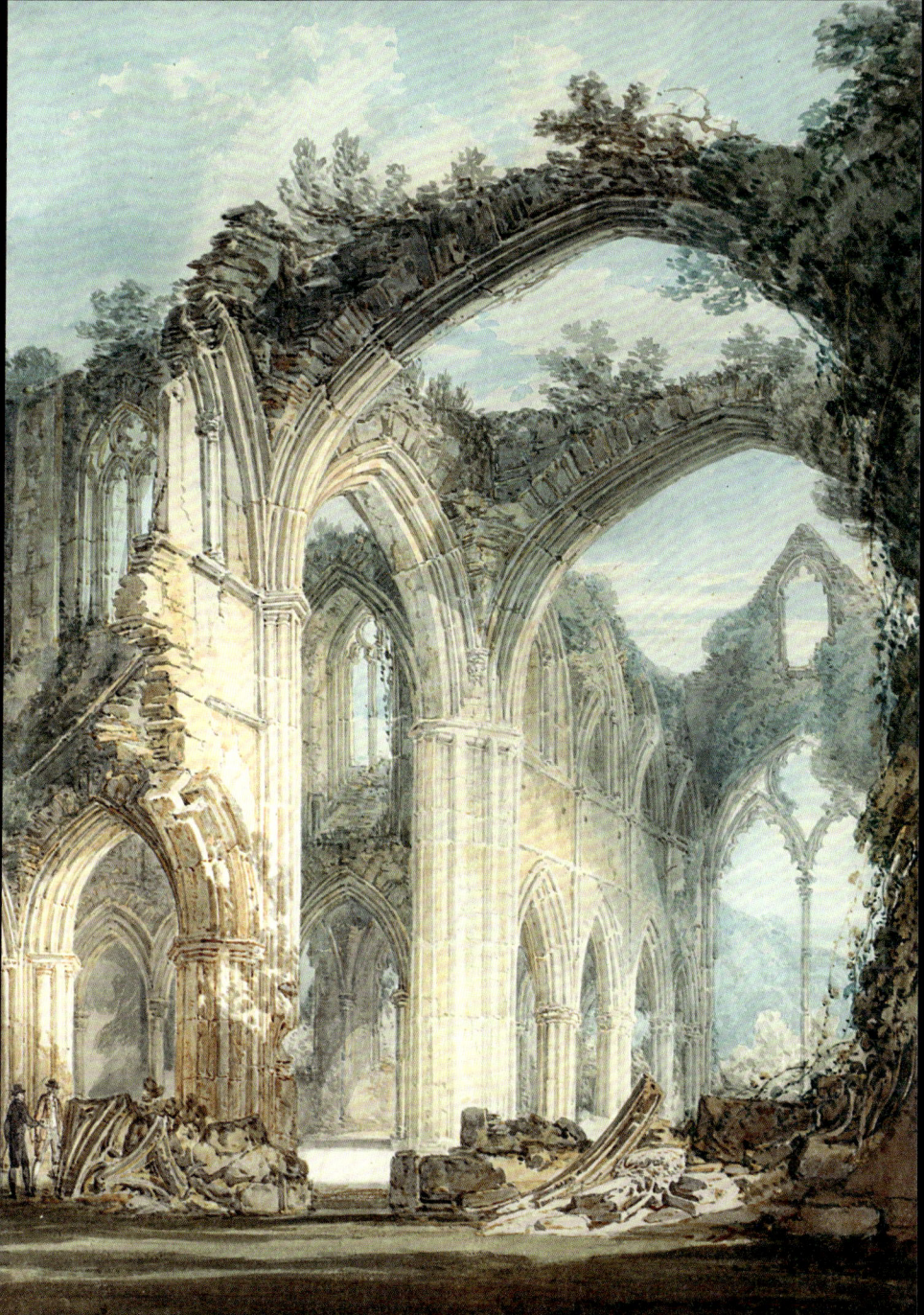

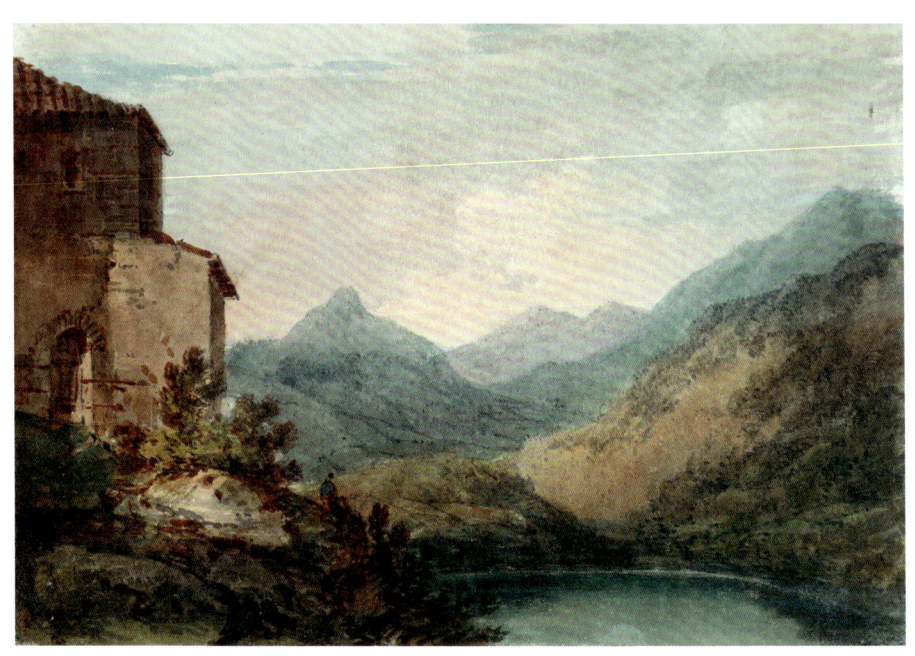

A Building by a Lake among
Mountains at Tigues, on the
Route to Mount Cenis c.1796
Pencil and watercolour
on paper
17.4 × 24.7

An Old Woman in a Cottage
Kitchen ('Internal of a Cottage,
a Study at Ely') exh.1796
Pencil and watercolour
on paper
20.4 × 27

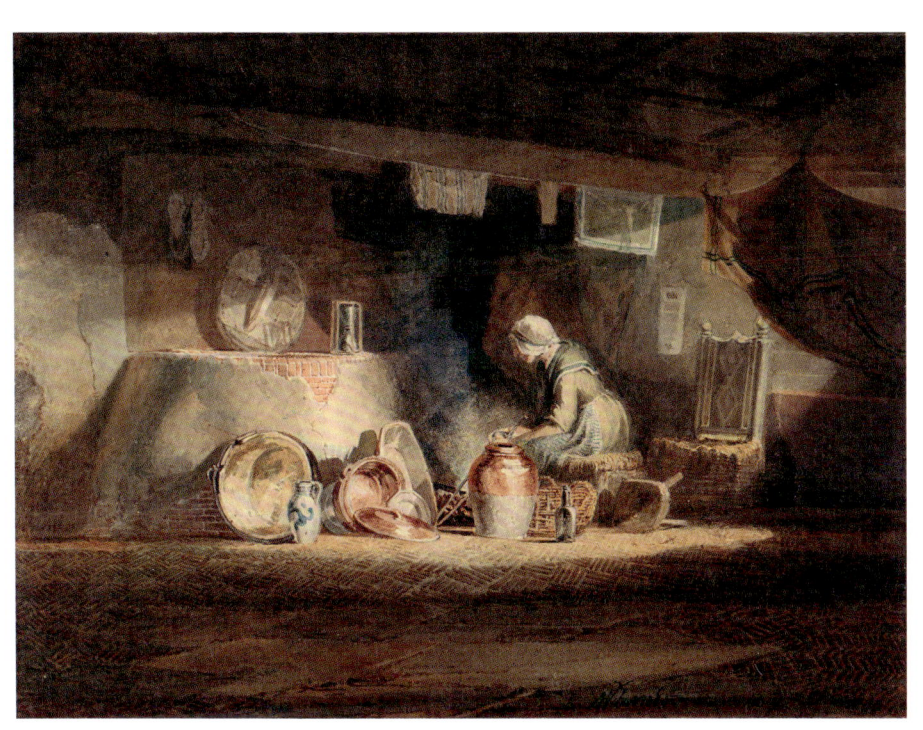

OVERLEAF
Fishermen at Sea
exh.1796
Oil paint on canvas
91.4 × 122.2

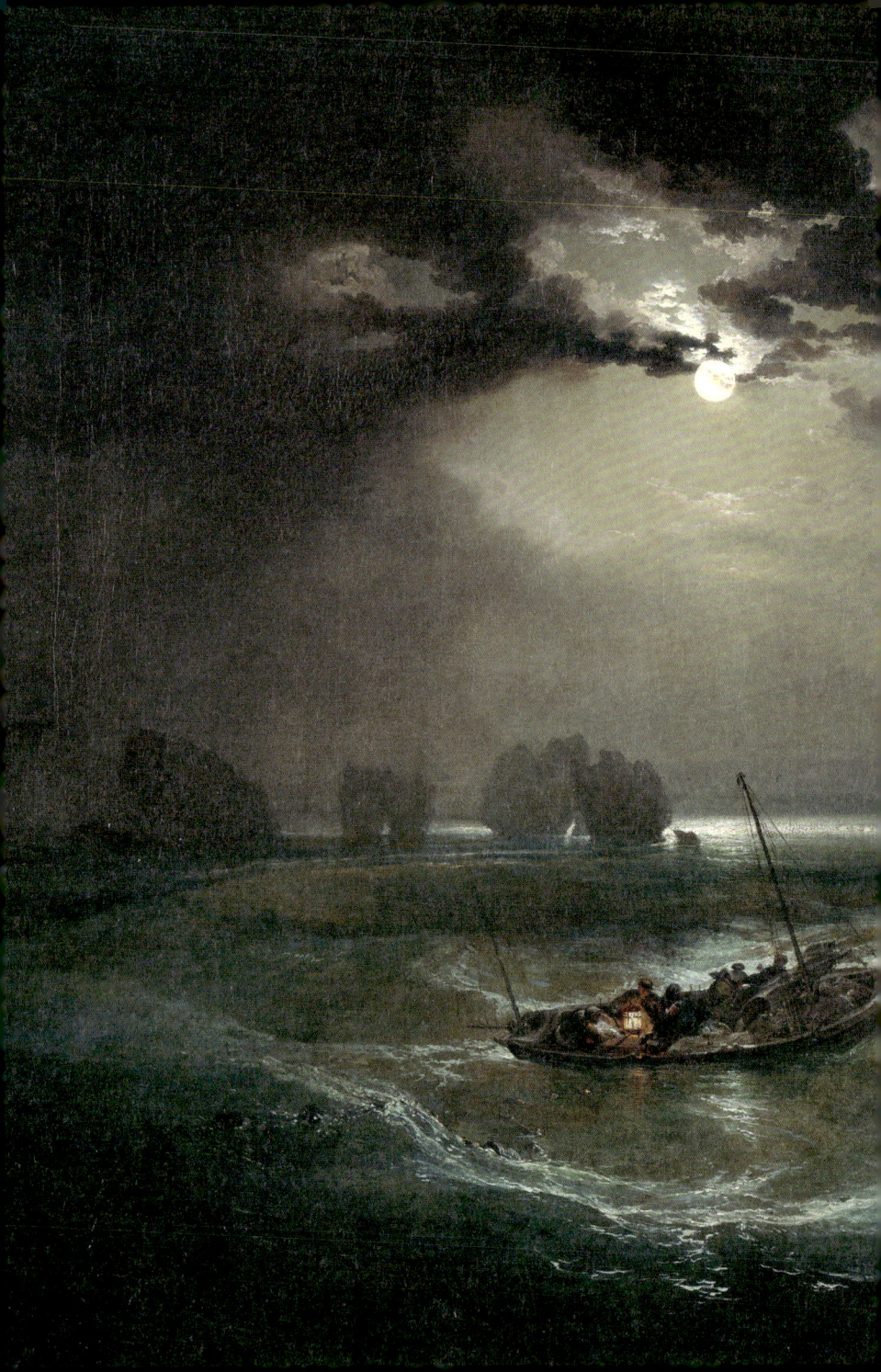

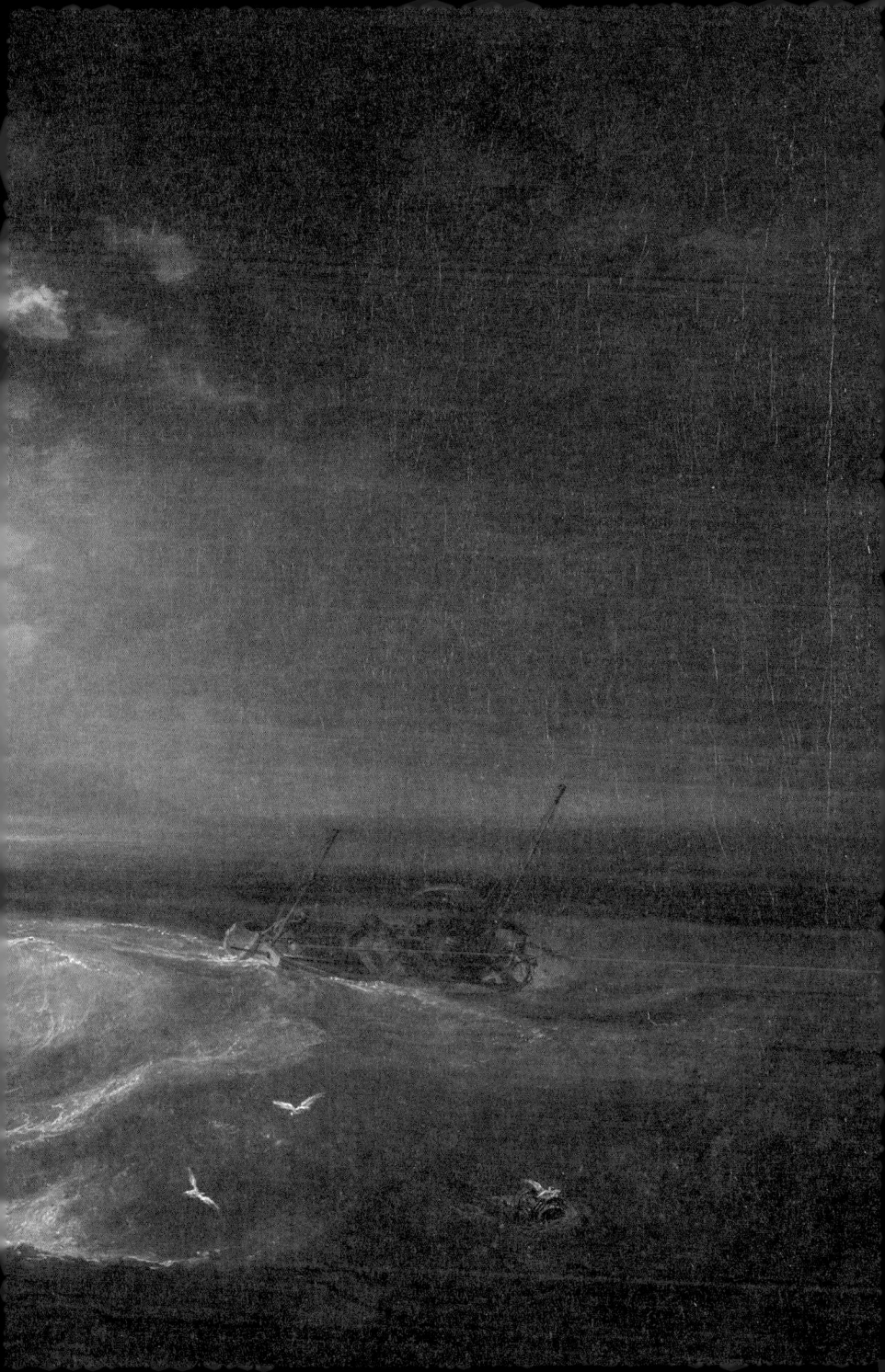

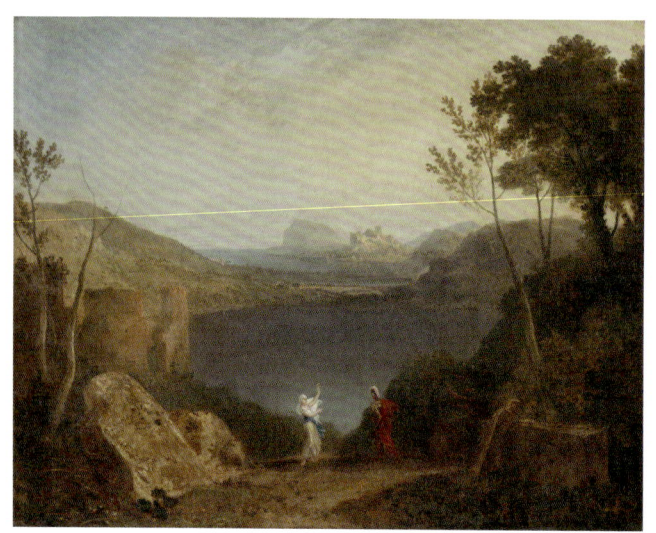

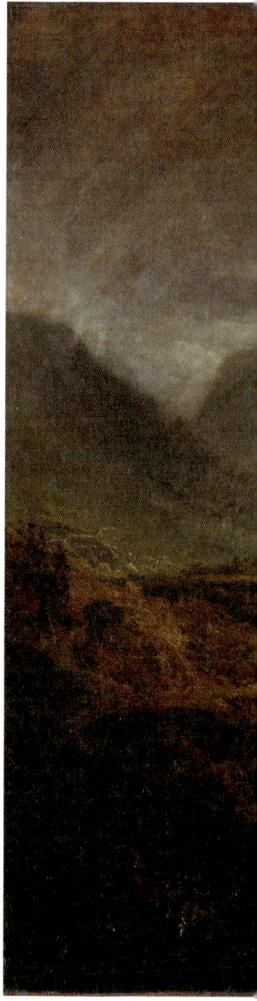

ABOVE
*Aeneas and the Sibyl, Lake
Avernus* c.1798
Oil paint on canvas
76.5 × 98.4

*Buttermere Lake, with part
of Cromackwater, Cumberland,
a shower* exh.1798
Oil paint on canvas
88.9 × 119.4

First exhibited with the lines:

Till in the western sky the downward sun
Looks out effulgent – the rapid radiance
instantaneous strikes
Th' illumin'd mountains – in a yellow mist
Bestriding the earth – the grand ethereal bow
Shoots up immense, and every hue unfolds.

– James Thomson, *The Seasons*

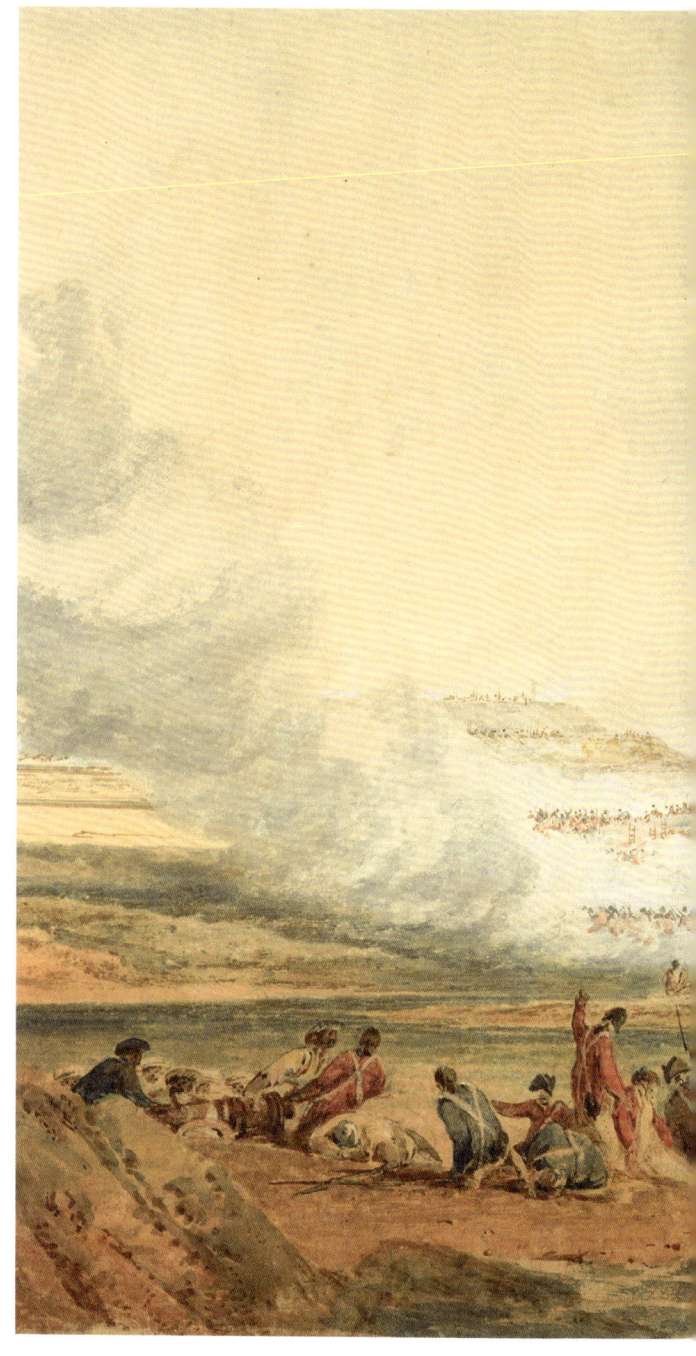

The Siege of Seringapatam
c.1800
Pencil, watercolour and
gouache on paper
42.1 × 64.7

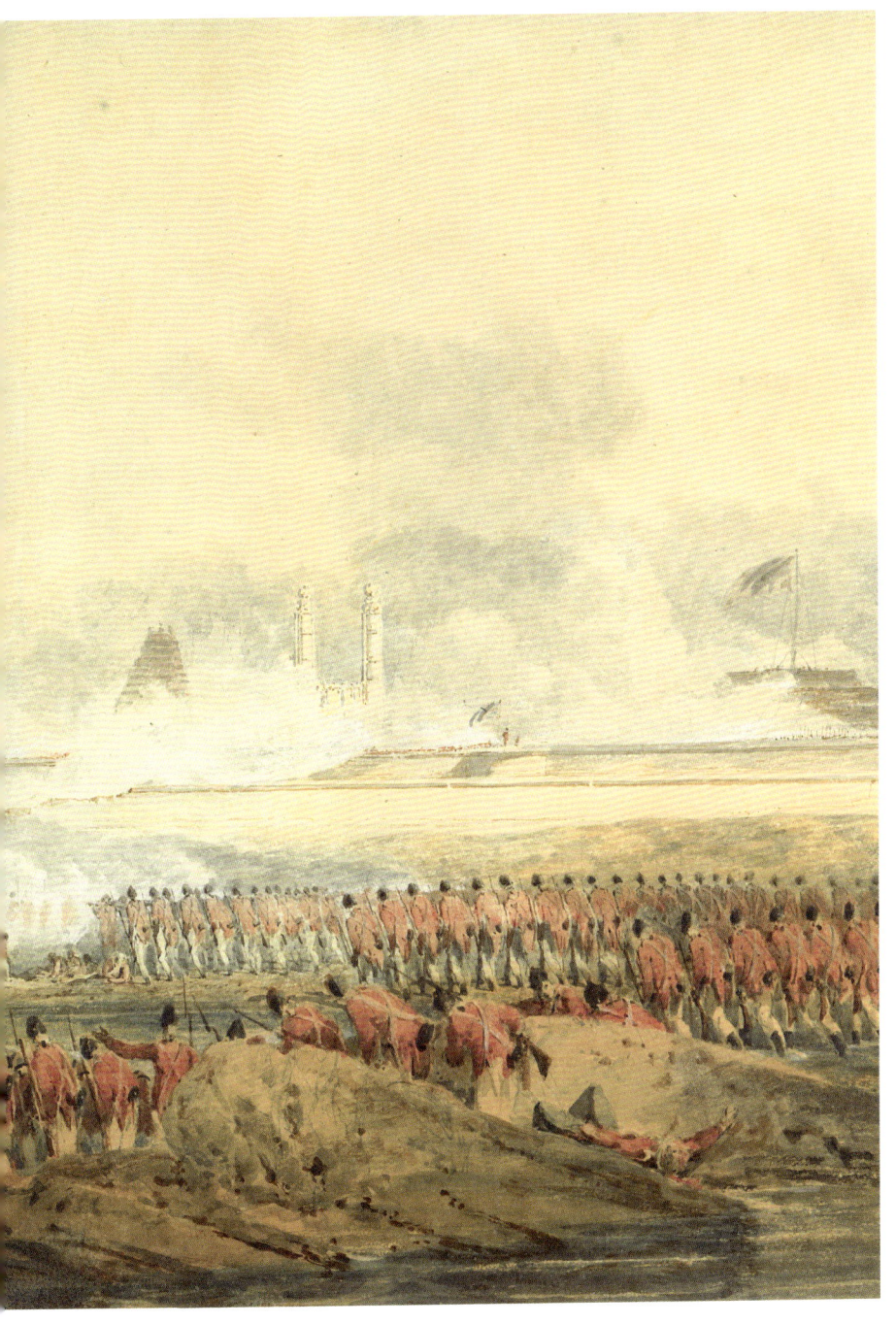

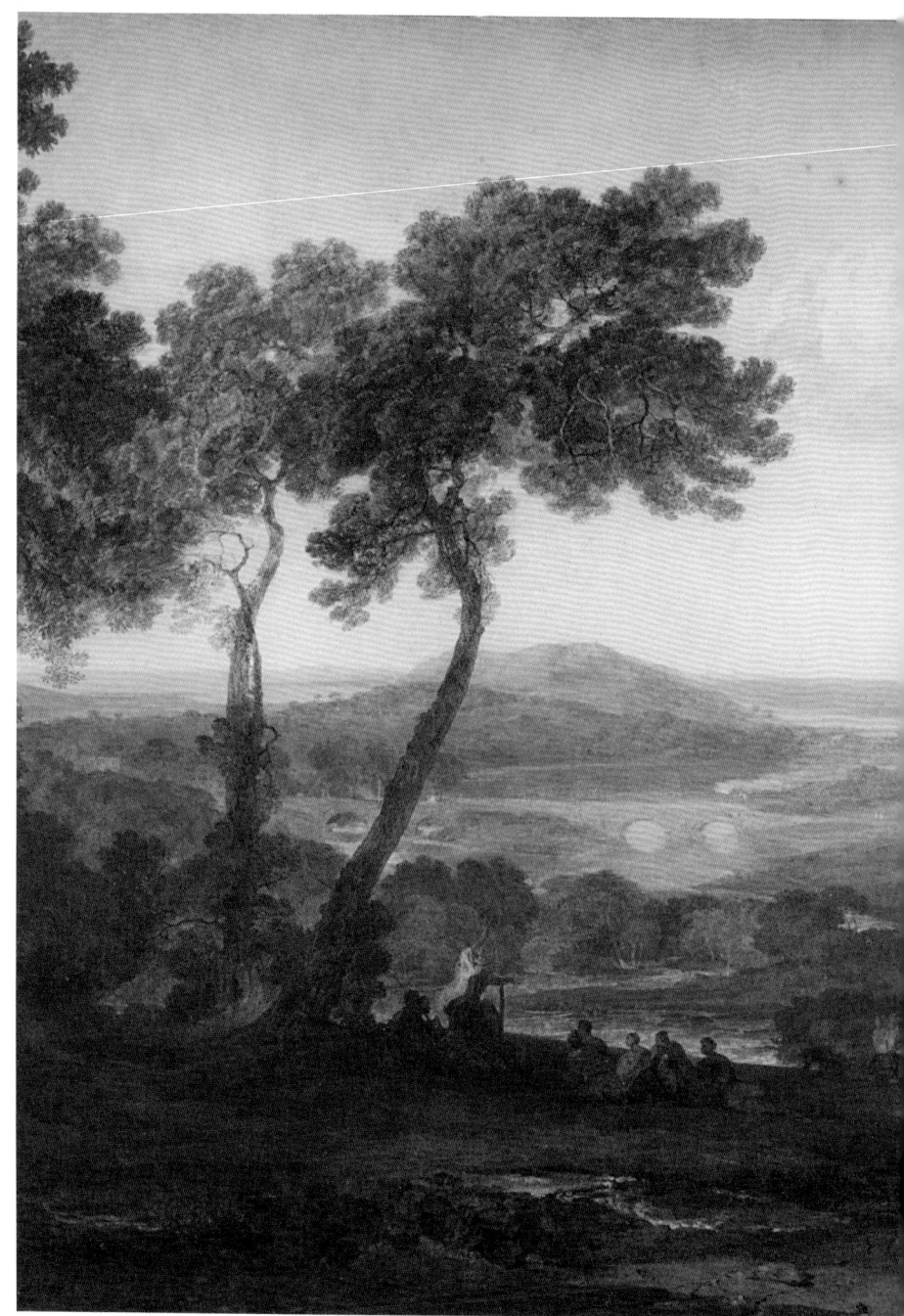

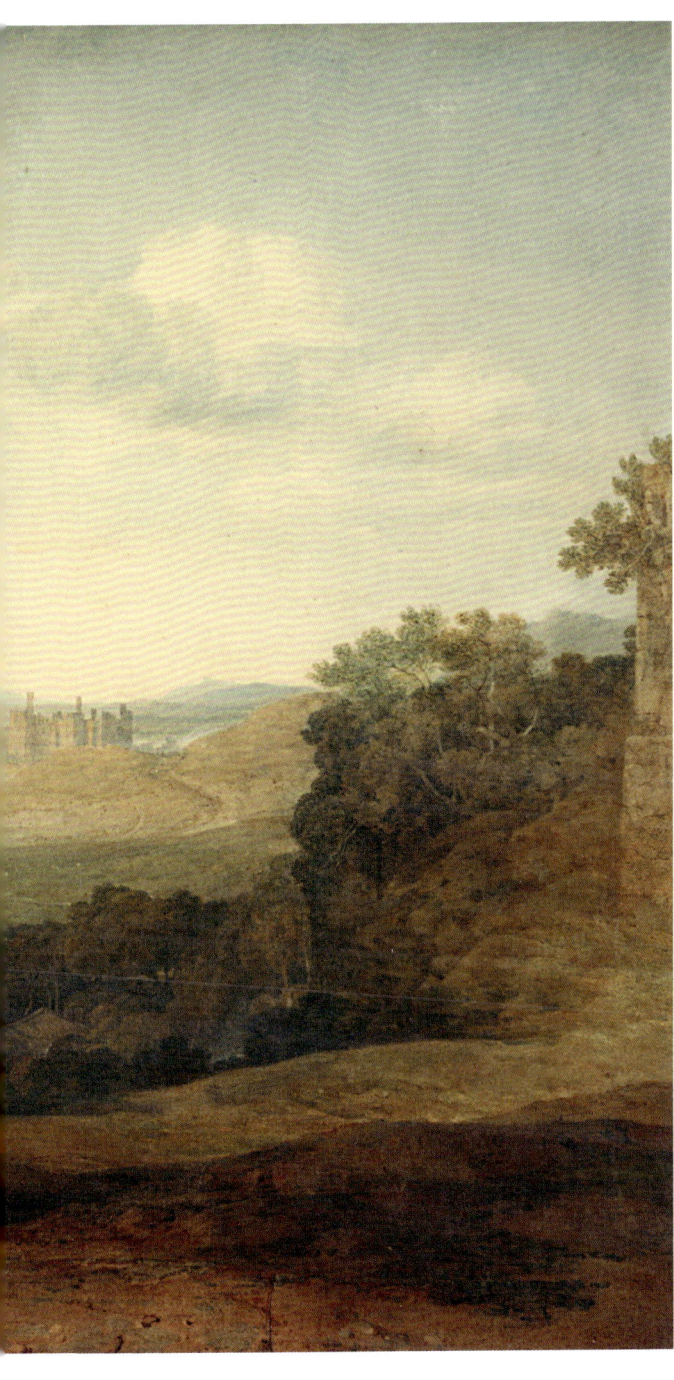

Caernarvon Castle, North Wales exh.1800
Pencil and watercolour with gum Arabic on paper, mounted on board
56.3 × 99.4

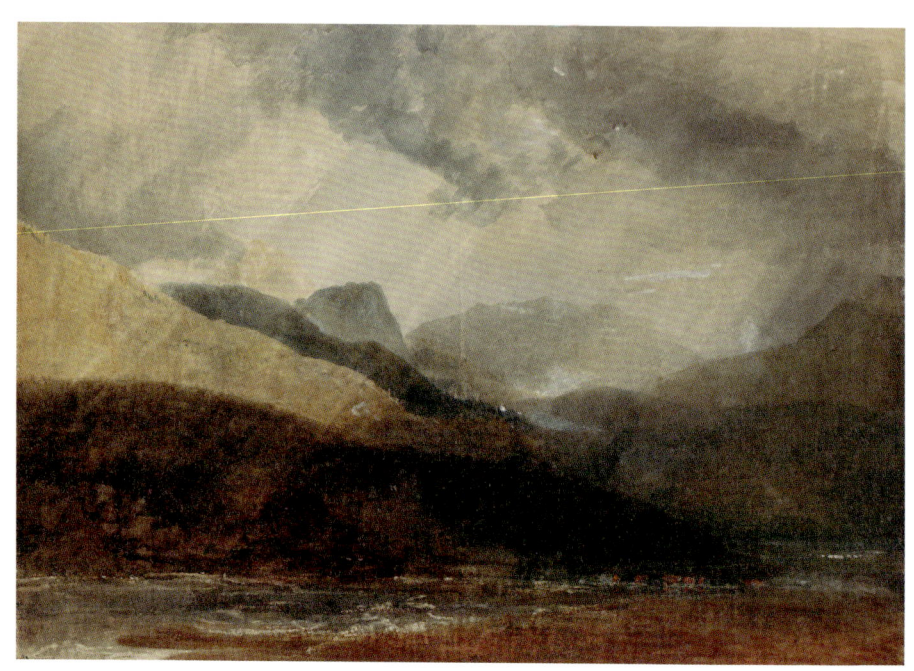

*Blair Atholl, Looking towards
Killiecrankie* c.1801–2
Watercolour and gouache
on paper
53.3 × 78

*The Schöllenen Gorge from
the Devil's Bridge, Pass of St
Gotthard* 1802
Pencil, watercolour and
gouache on paper prepared
with grey wash
47 × 31.4

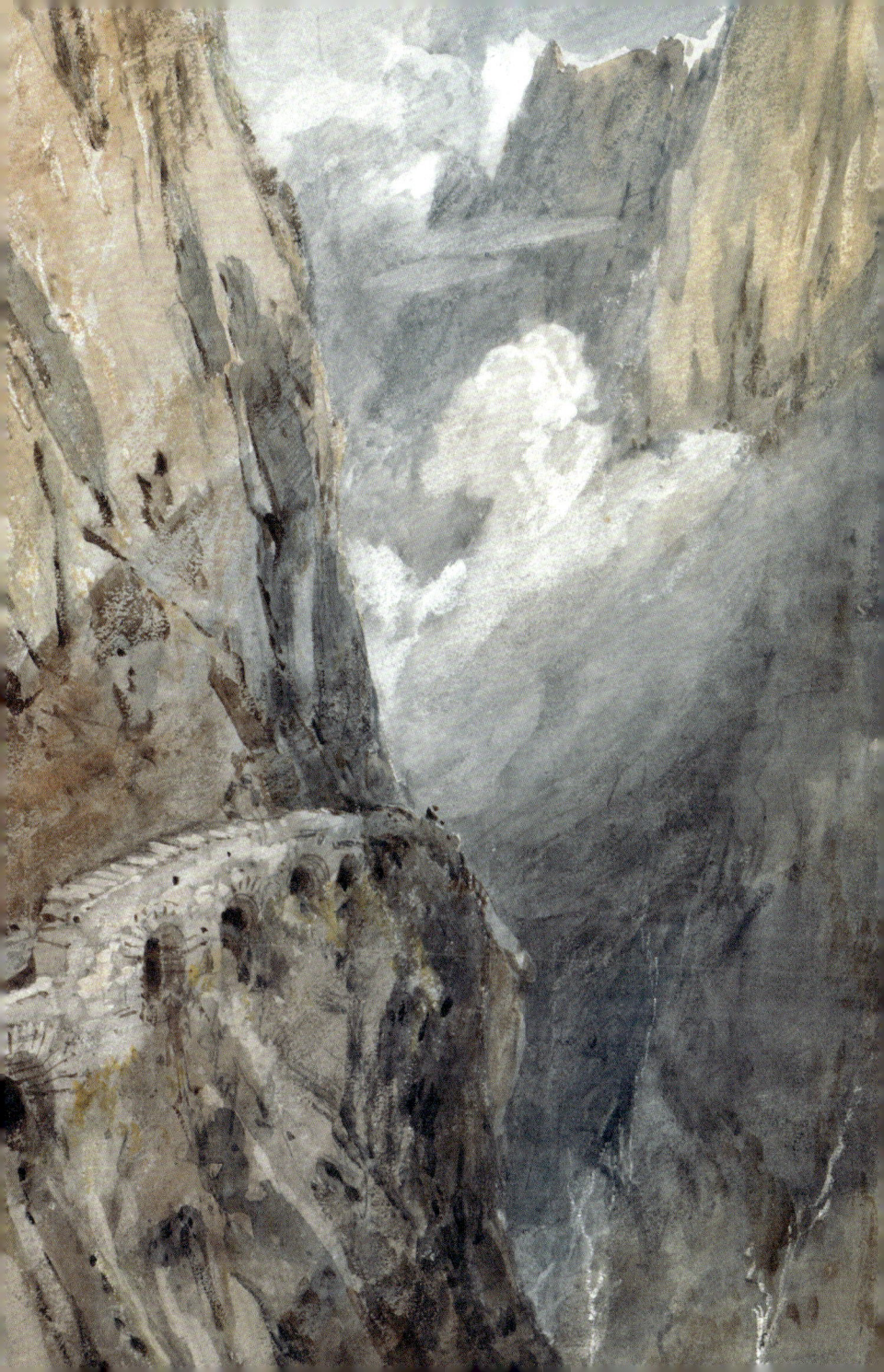

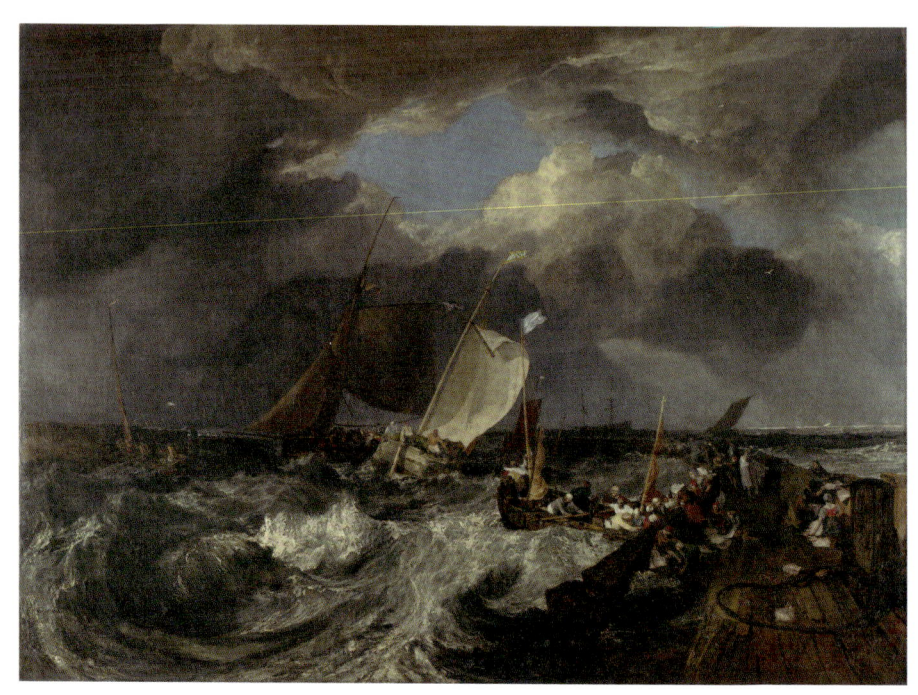

*Calais Pier, with French
Poissards preparing for sea;
an English packet arriving*
exh.1803
Oil paint on canvas
172 × 240

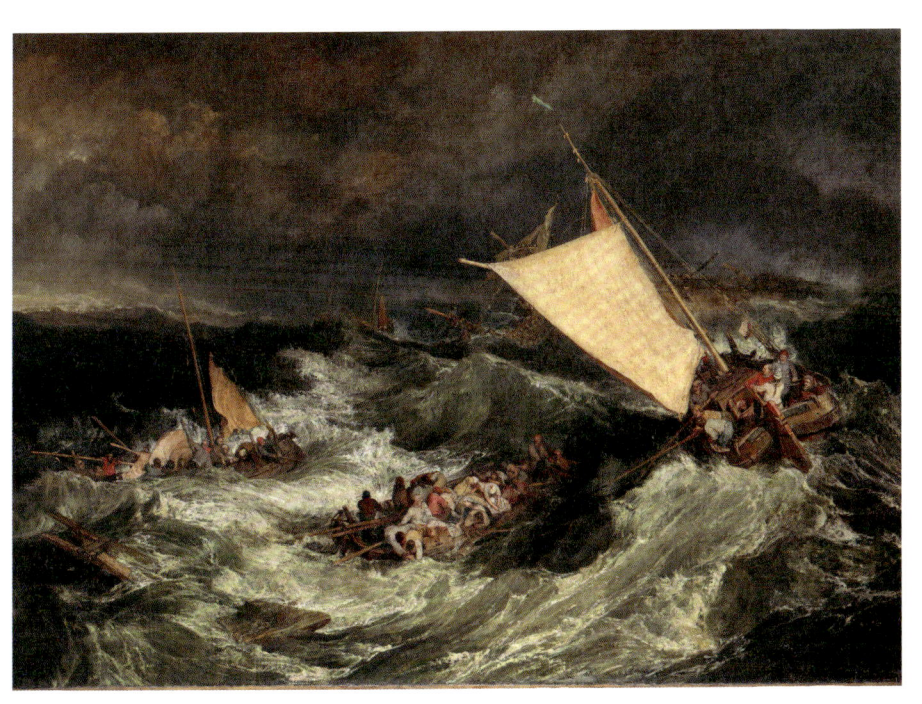

The Shipwreck exh.1805
Oil paint on canvas
170.5 × 241.6

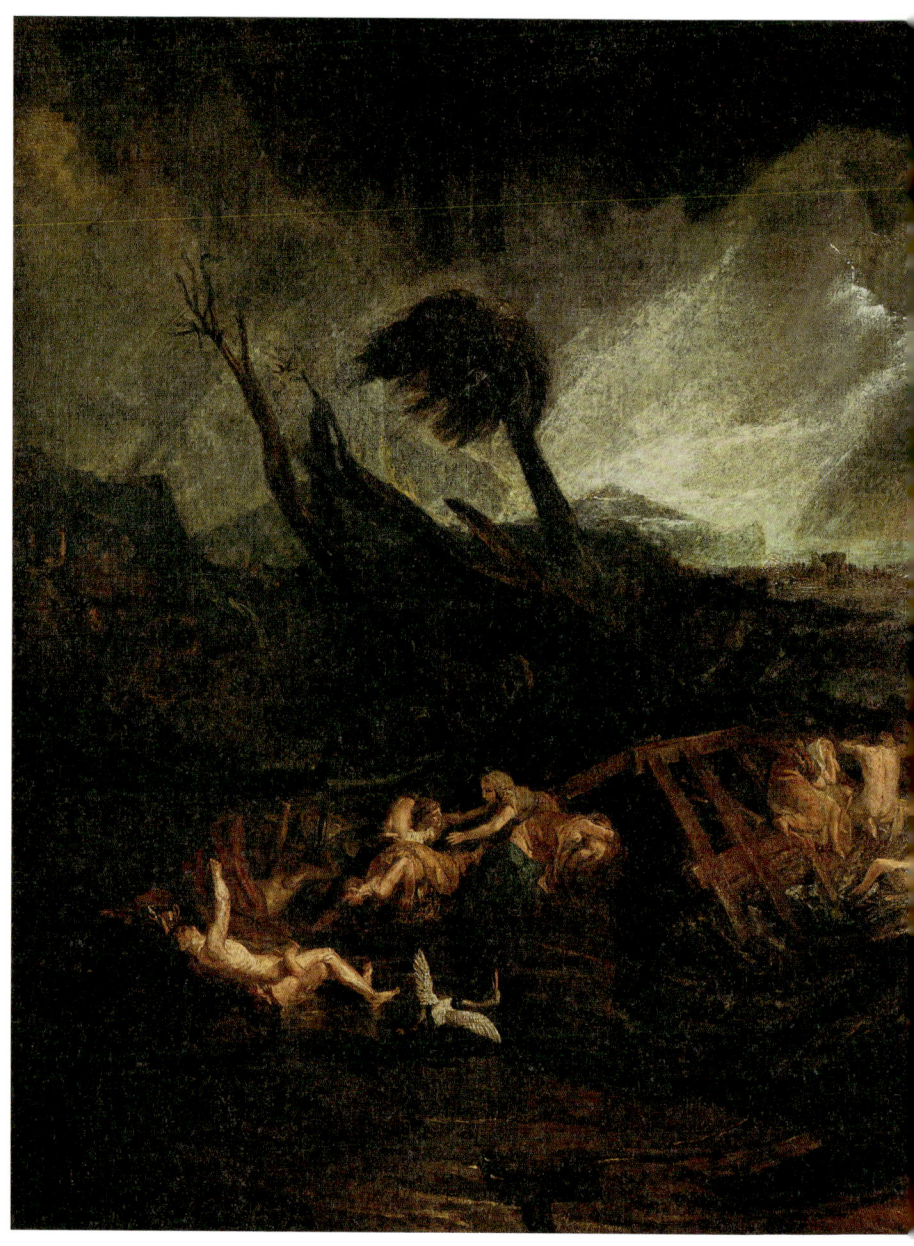

The Deluge ?exh.1805
Oil paint on canvas
142.9 × 235.6

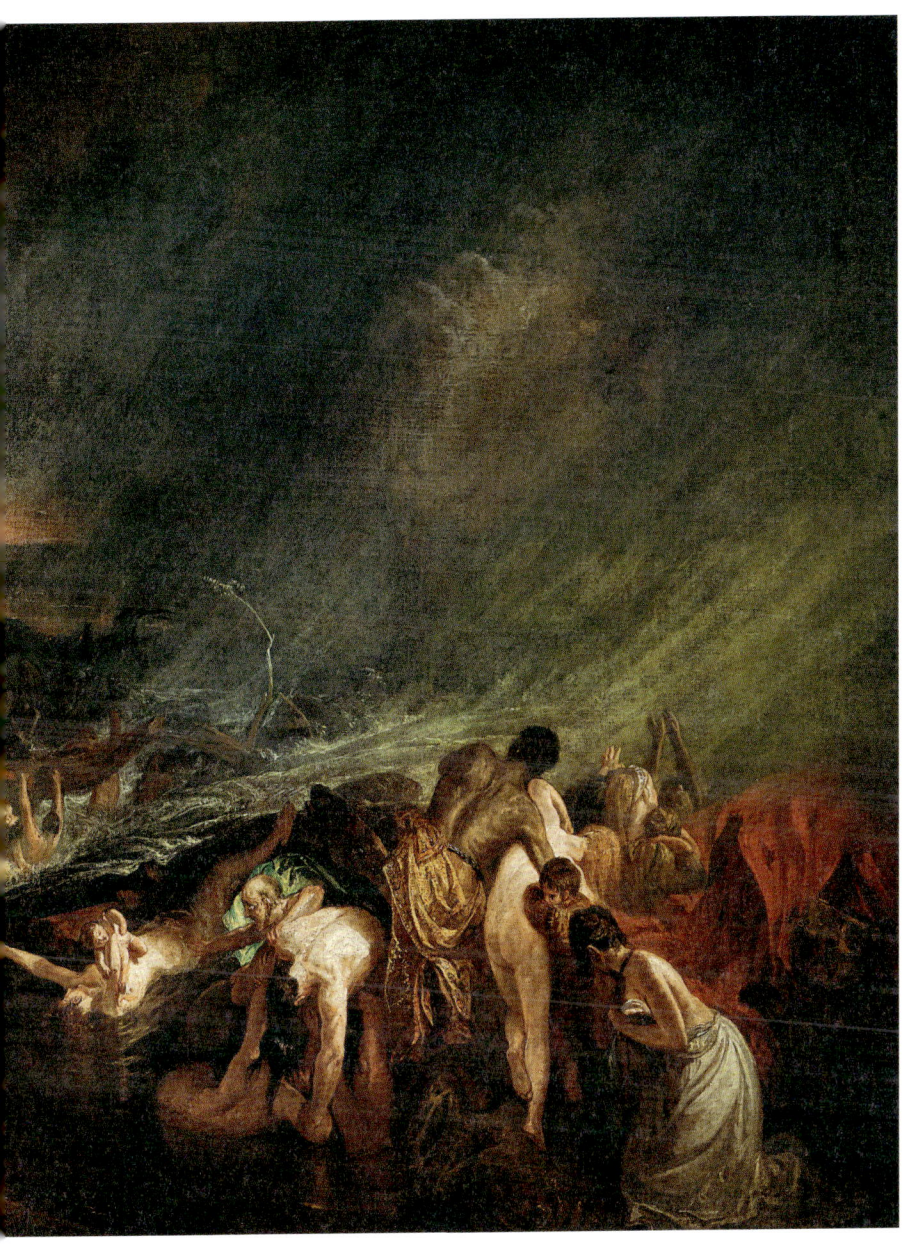

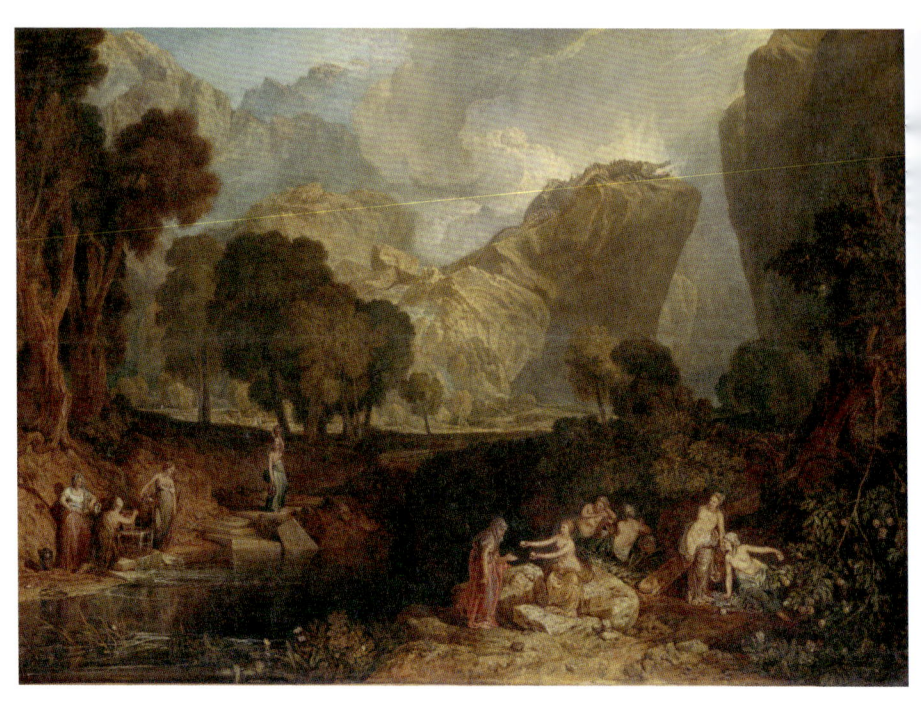

*The Goddess of Discord
Choosing the Apple of
Contention in the Garden
of the Hesperides* exh.1806
Oil paint on canvas
155.3 × 218.4

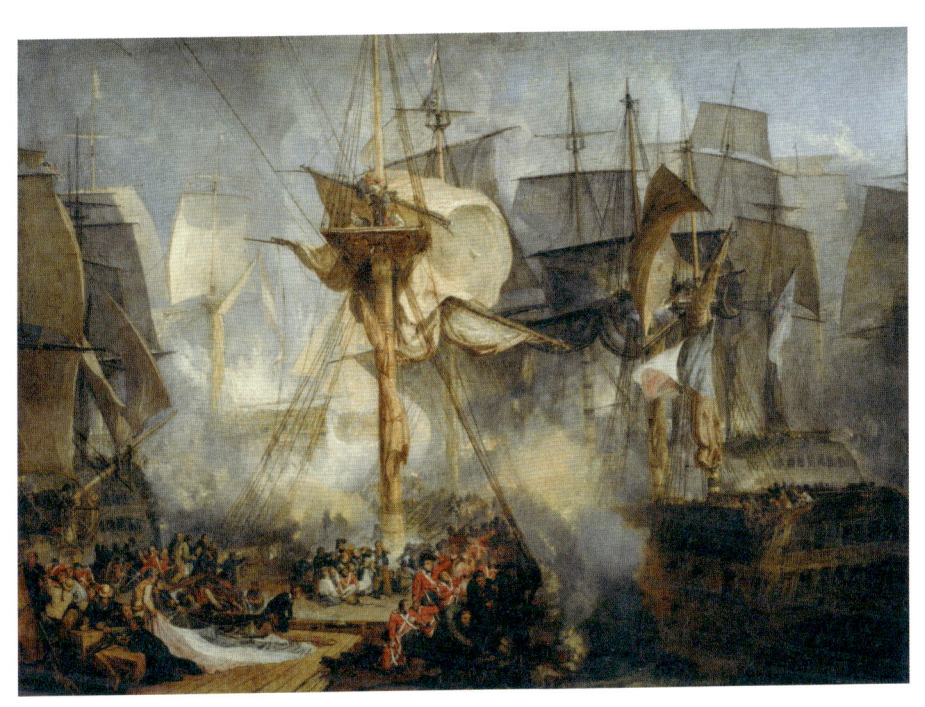

*The Battle of Trafalgar, as
seen from the Mizen Starboard
Shrouds of the Victory*
exh.1806, reworked 1808
Oil paint on canvas
170.8 × 238.8

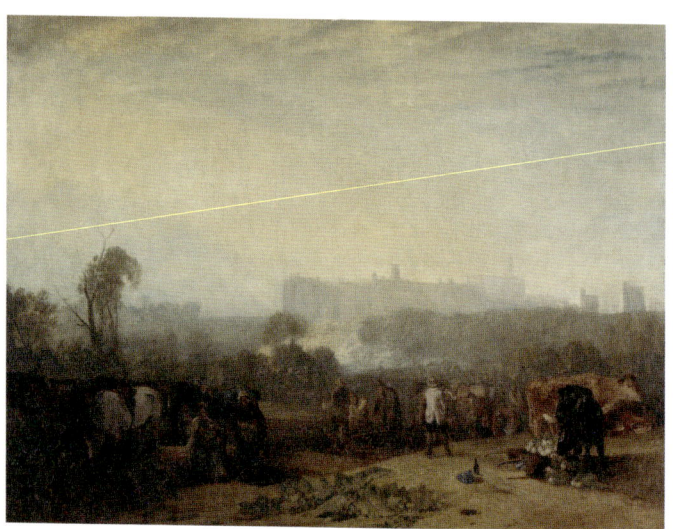

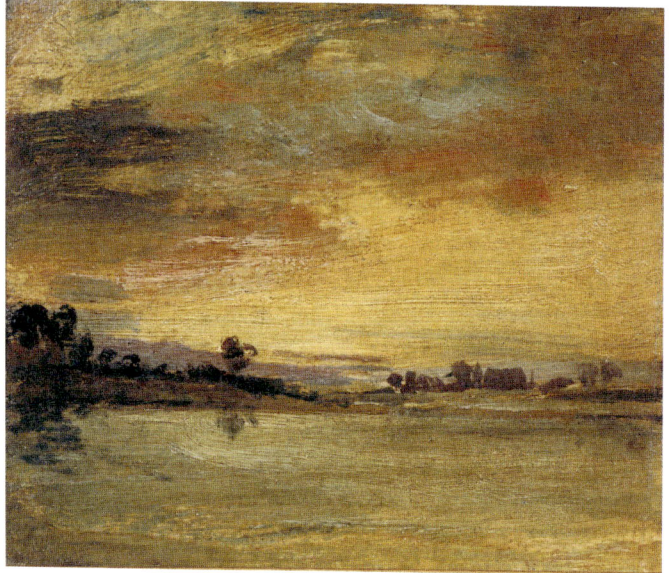

Ploughing up Turnips near
Slough ('Windsor') exh.1809
Oil paint on canvas
101.9 × 130.2

Sunset on the River 1805
Oil paint on mahogany
veneer on wooden panel
15.6 × 18.7

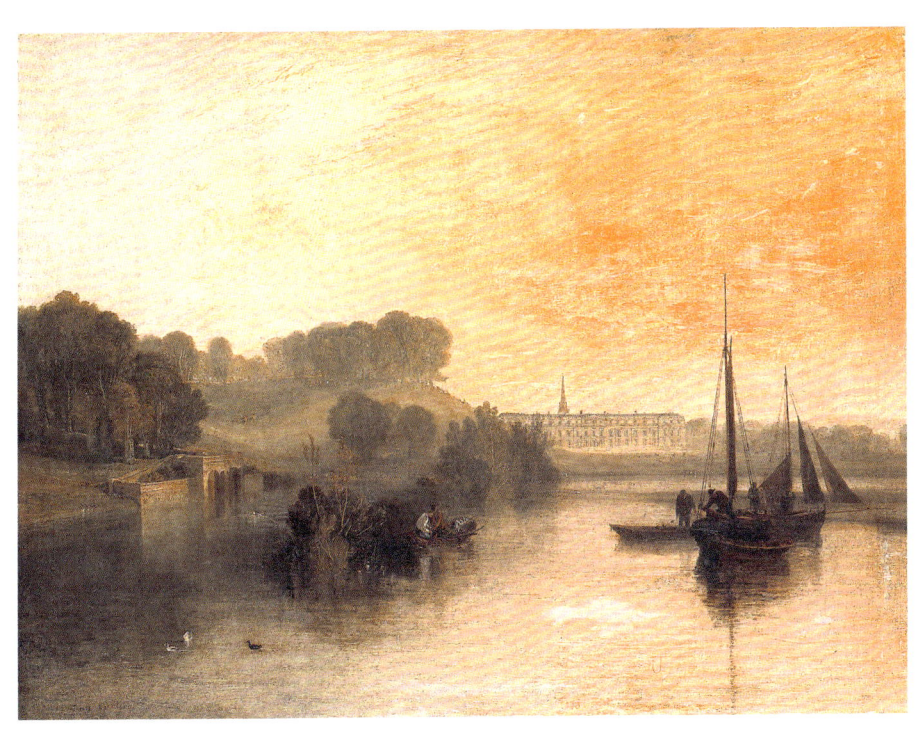

*Petworth, Sussex, the Seat
of the Earl of Egremont:
Dewy Morning* exh. 1810
Oil paint on canvas
91.4 × 120.6

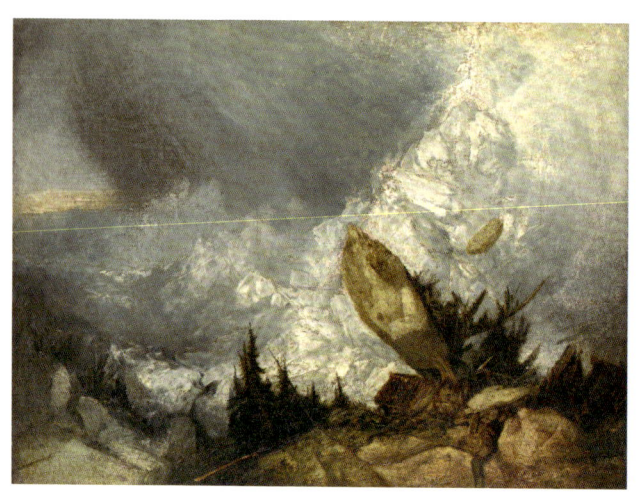

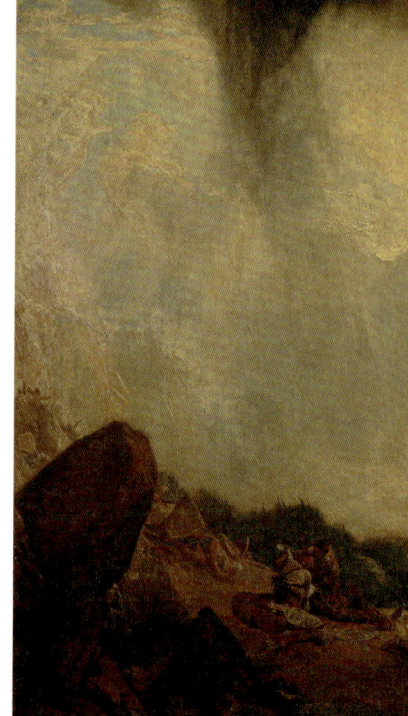

The Fall of an Avalanche
in the Grisons exh.1810
Oil paint on canvas
90.2 × 120

Snow Storm: Hannibal and
his Army Crossing the Alps
exh.1812
Oil paint on canvas
146 × 237.5

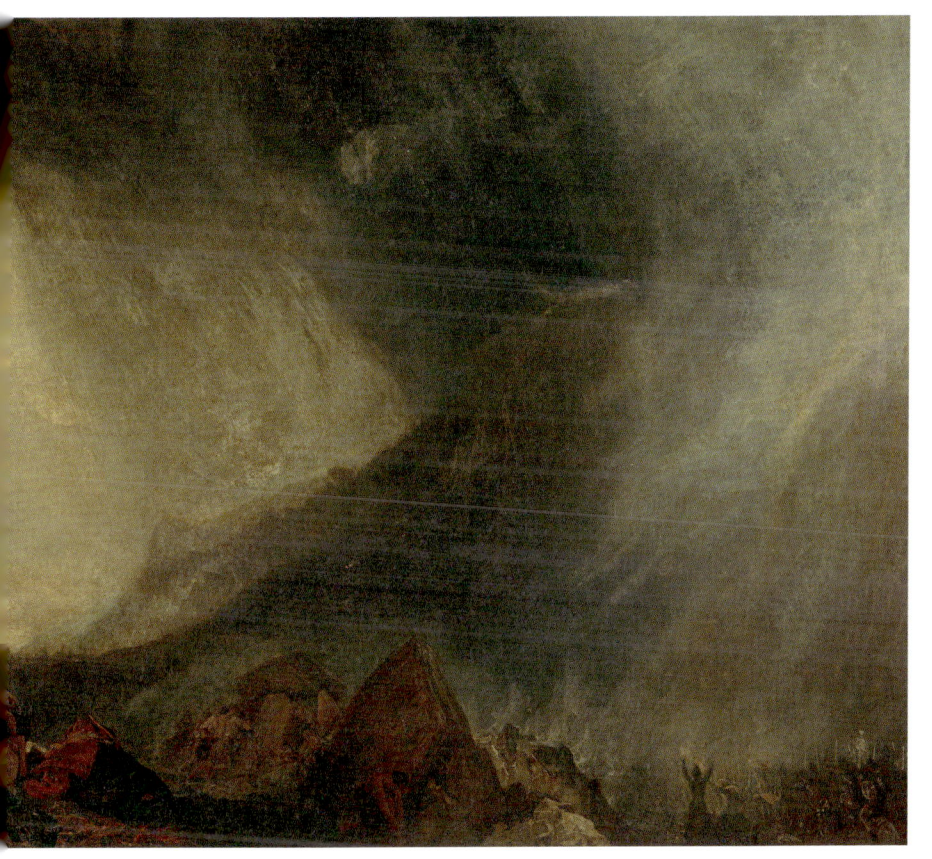

*St Mawes at the Pilchard
Season*, exh.1812
Oil paint on canvas
91.1 × 120.6

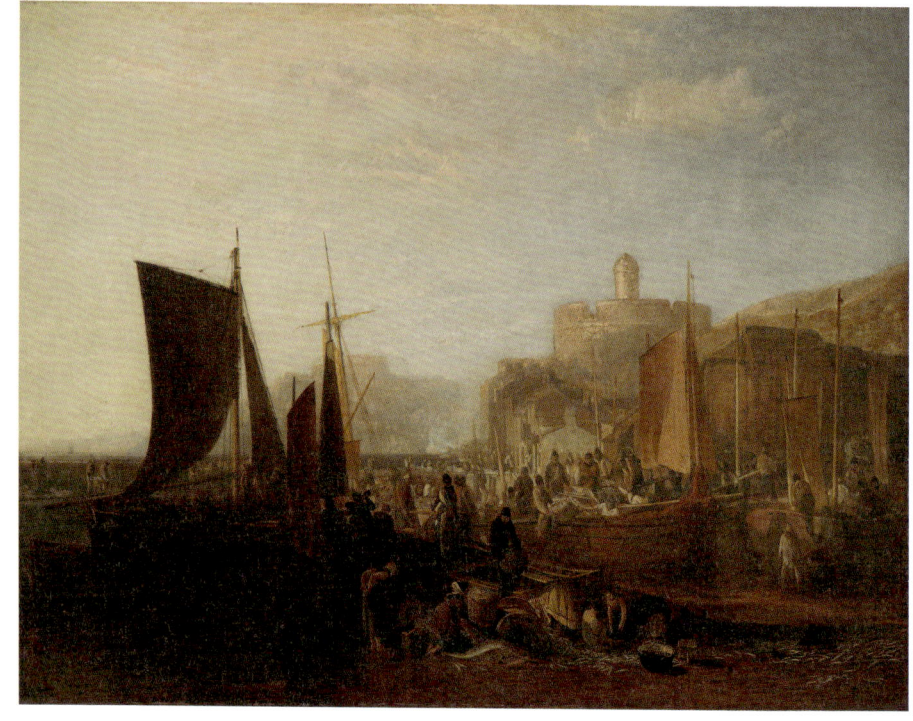

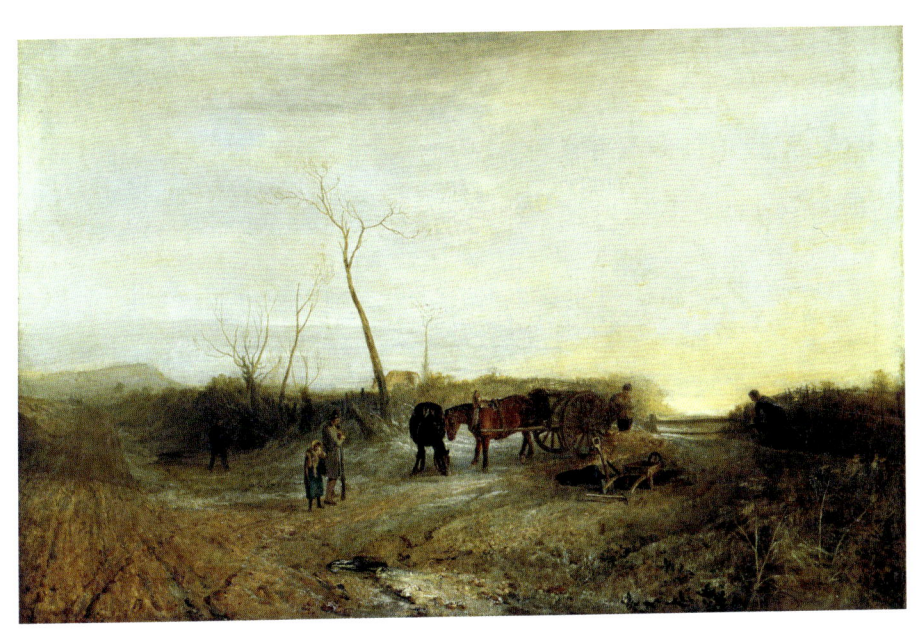

Frosty Morning, exh.1813
Oil paint on canvas
113.7 × 174.6

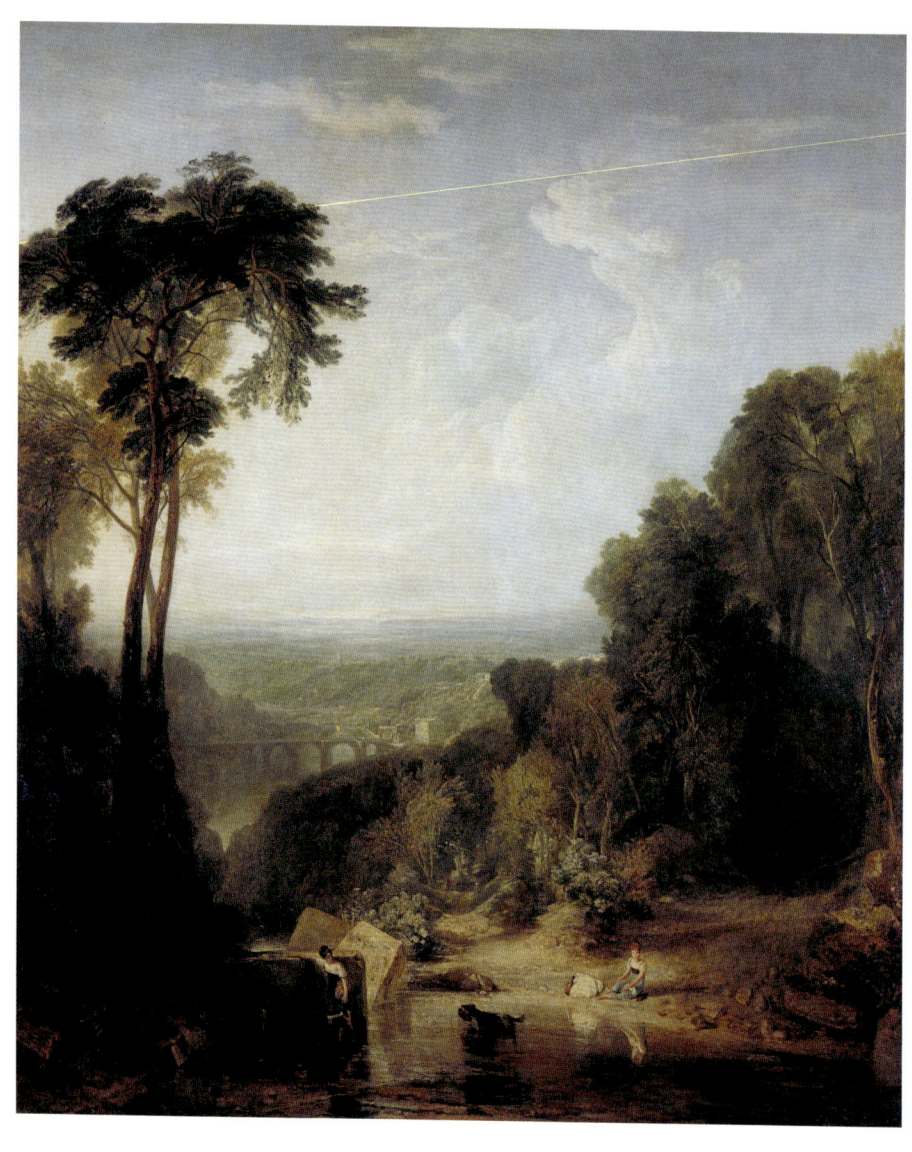

Crossing the Brook, exh.1815
Oil paint on canvas
193 × 165.1

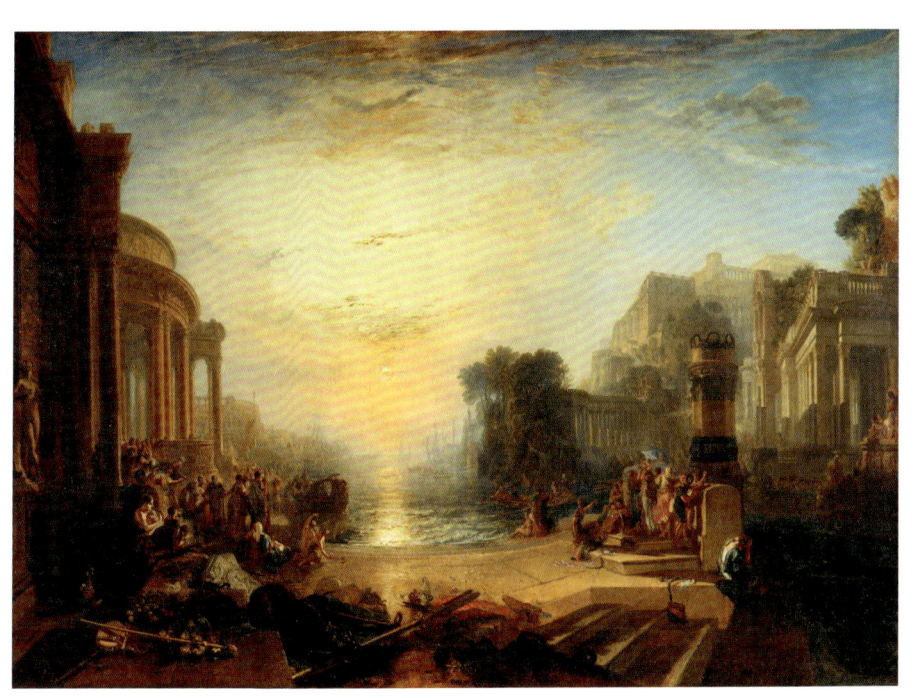

*The Decline of the Carthaginian Empire –
Rome being determined on the Overthrow
of her Hated Rival, demanded from her such
Terms as might either force her into War,
or ruin her by Compliance: the Enervated
Carthaginians, in their Anxiety for Peace,
consented to give up their Arms and their
Children exh.1817*
Oil paint on canvas
170.2 × 238.8

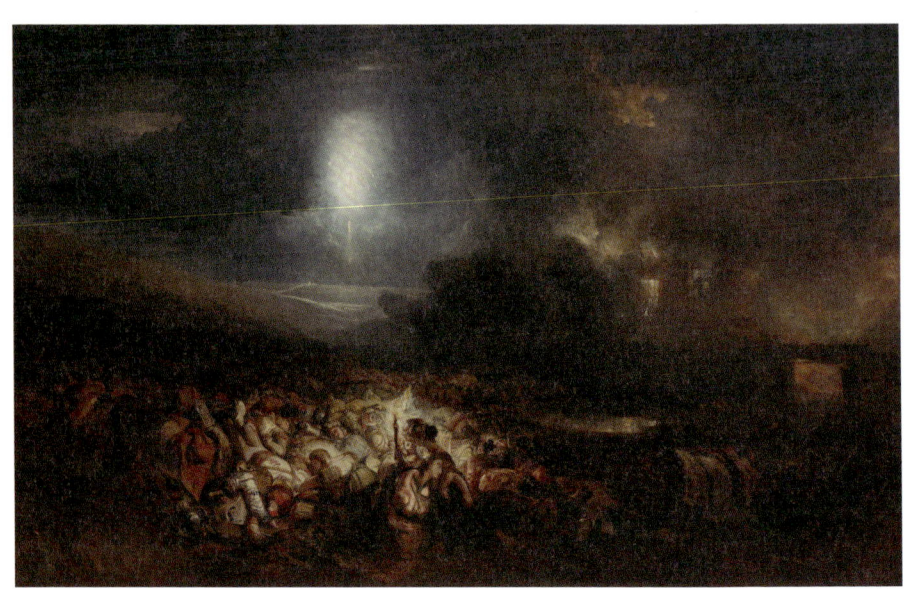

The Field of Waterloo
exh.1818
Oil paint on canvas
147.3 × 238.8

Entrance of the Meuse:
Orange-Merchant on the Bar,
going to Pieces; Brill Church
bearing S.E. *by* S., *Masensluys*
E. *by* S. exh.1819
Oil paint on canvas
174.3 × 246.4

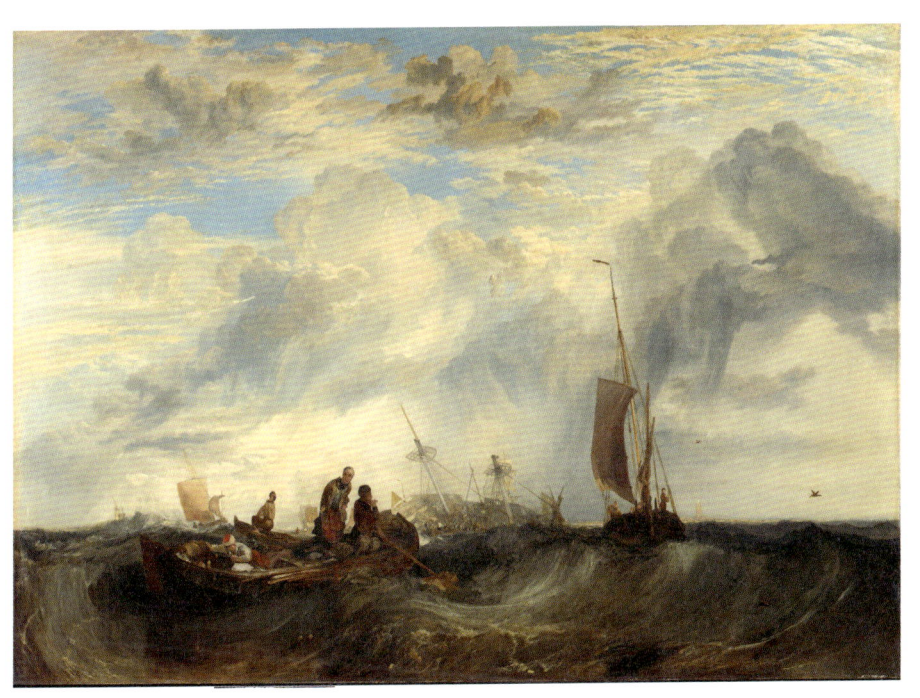

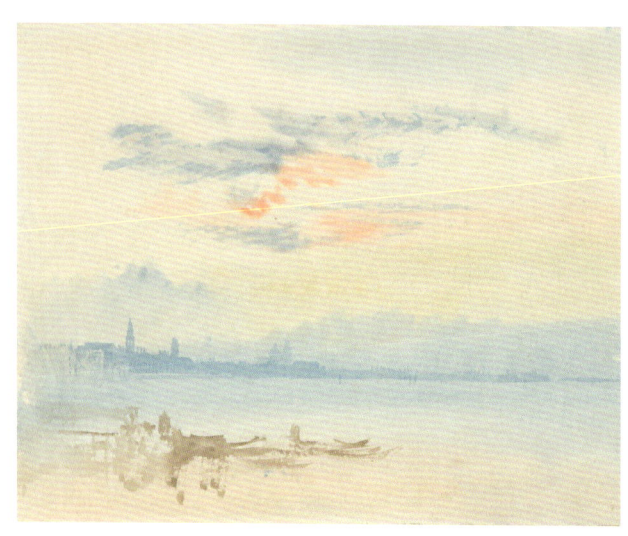

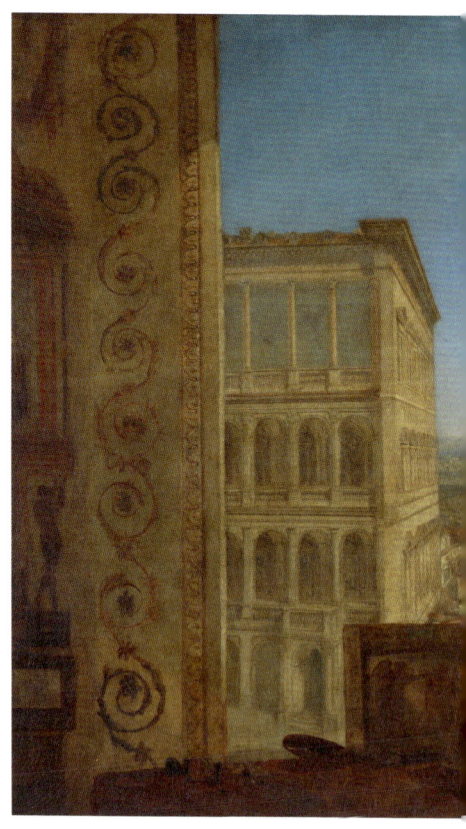

*Venice: Looking East towards
San Pietro di Castello – Early
Morning 1819
Watercolour on paper
22.3 × 28.7*

*Rome from the Vatican.
Rafaelle, accompanied
by La Fornarina, preparing
his Pictures for the Decoration
of the Loggia exh.1820
Oil paint on canvas
177.2 × 335.3*

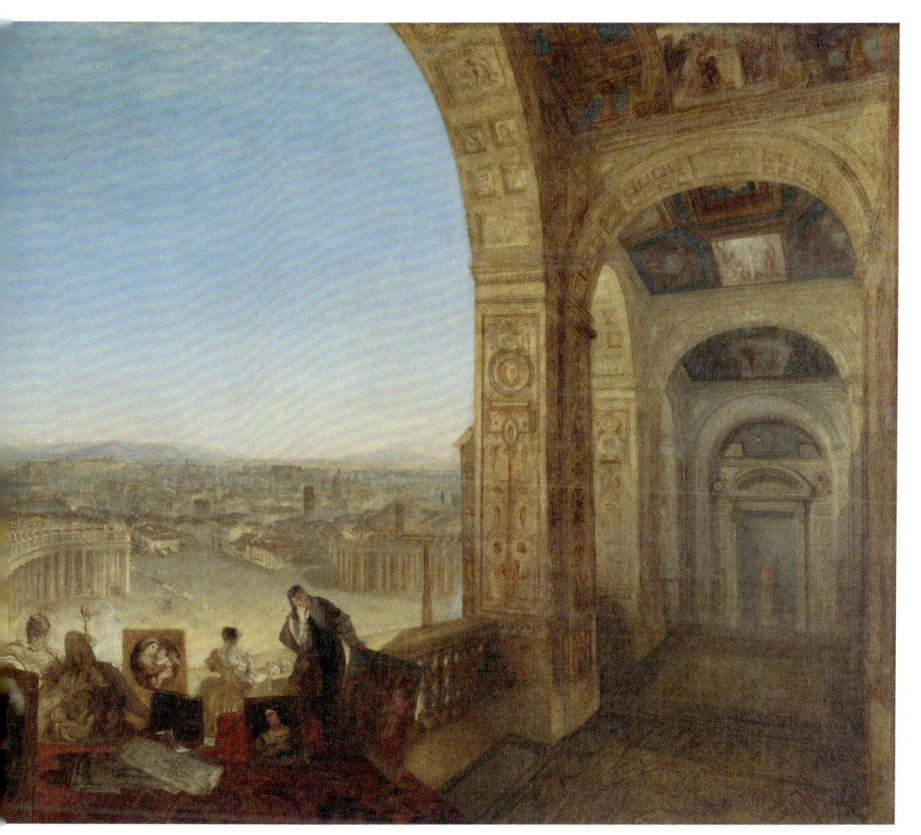

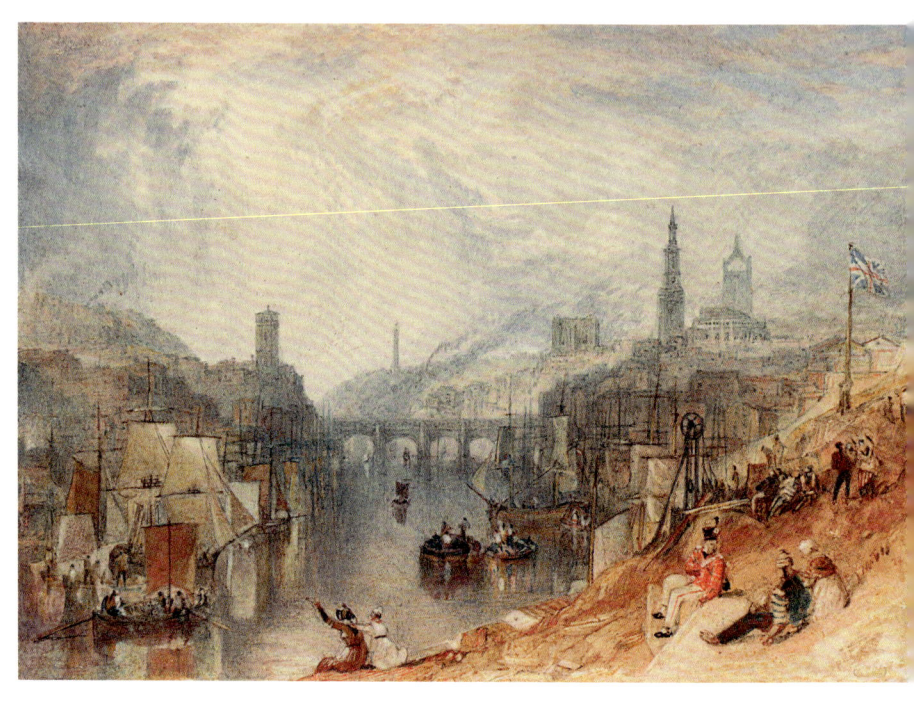

Newcastle-on-Tyne c.1823
Watercolour on paper
15.2 × 21.5

Whitby c.1824
Watercolour on paper
15.8 × 22.5

The Château, Nantes
c.1826–8
Watercolour, gouache
and ink on blue paper
12.9 × 18.3

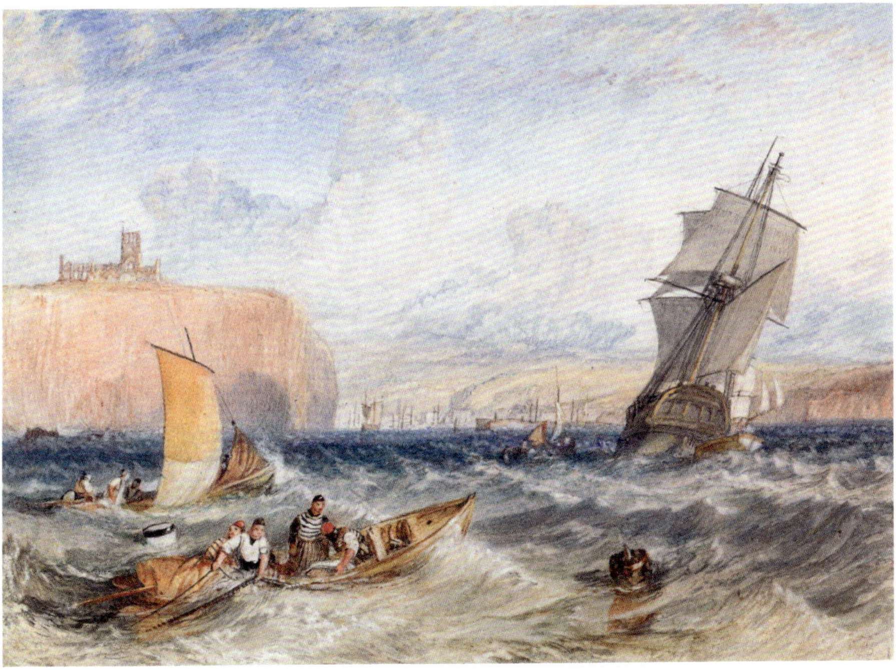

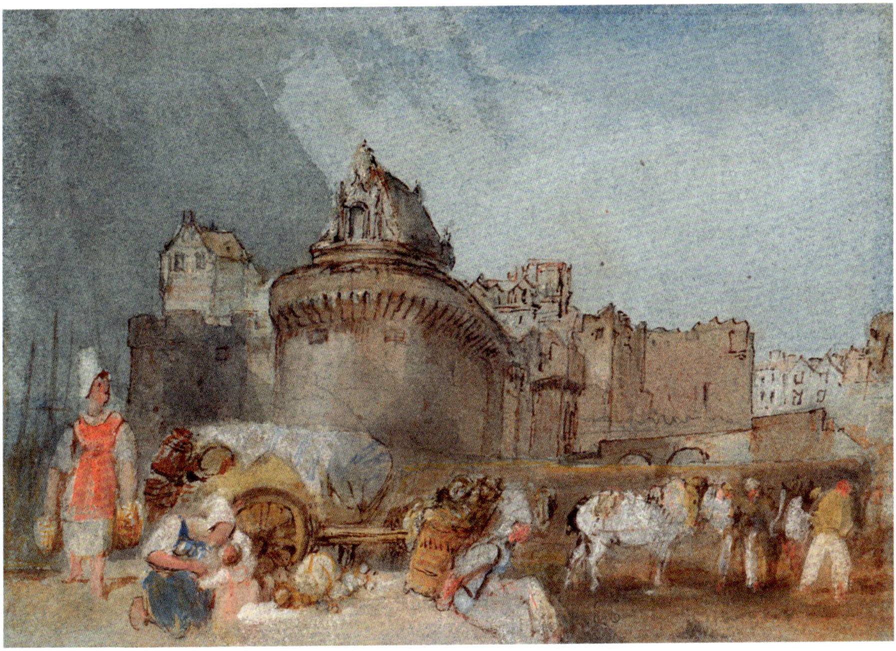

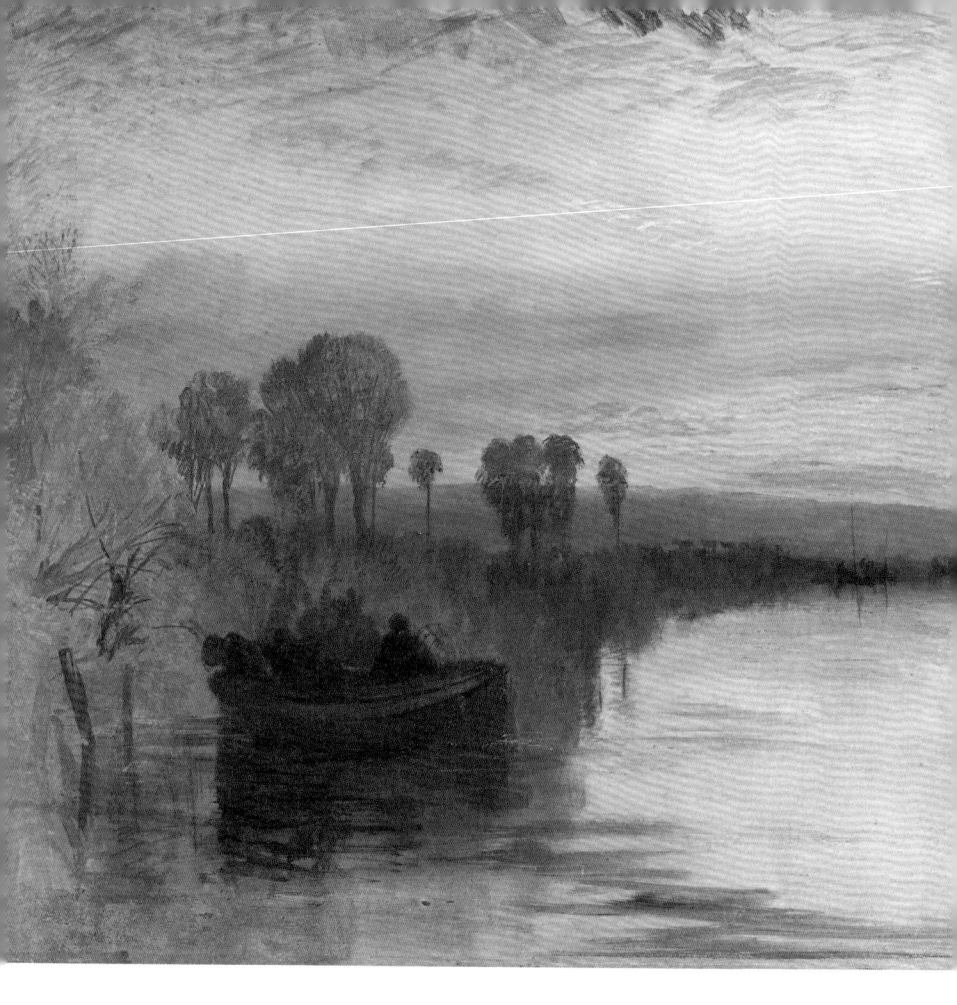

Chichester Canal c.1828
Oil paint on canvas
65.4 × 134.6

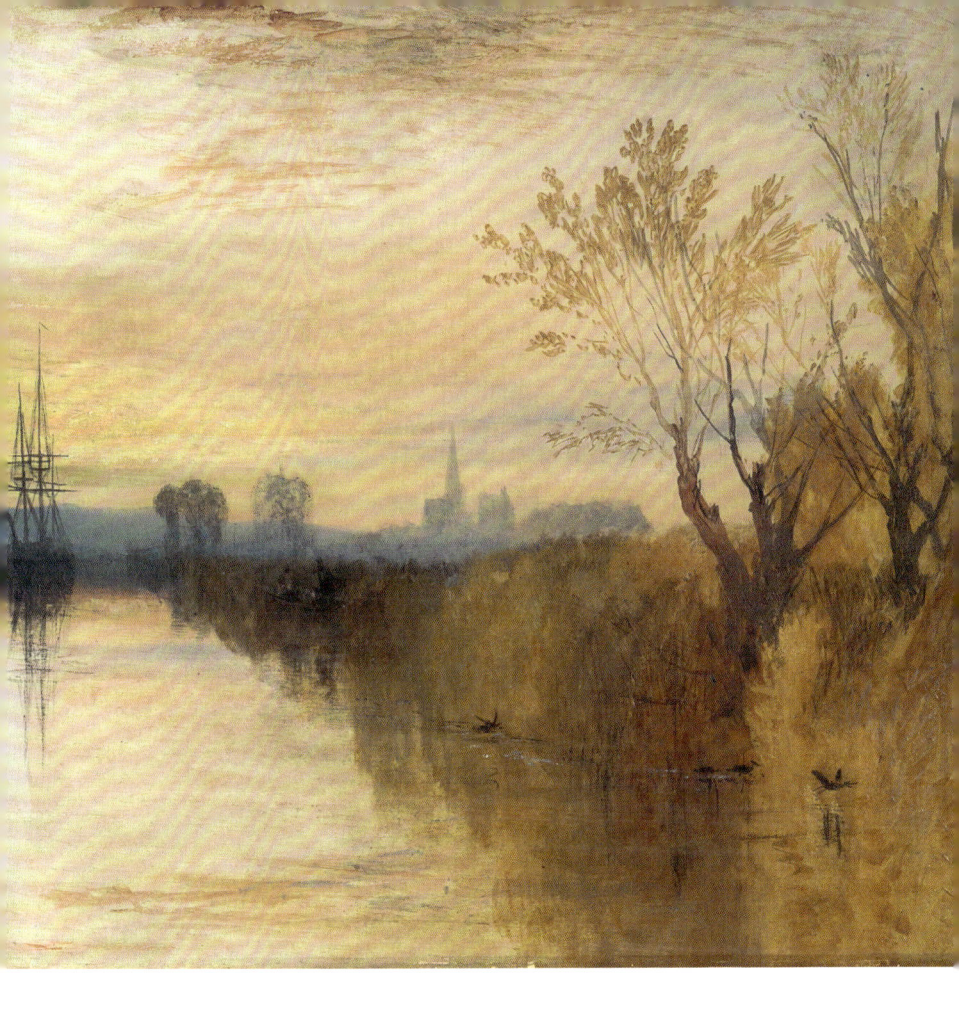

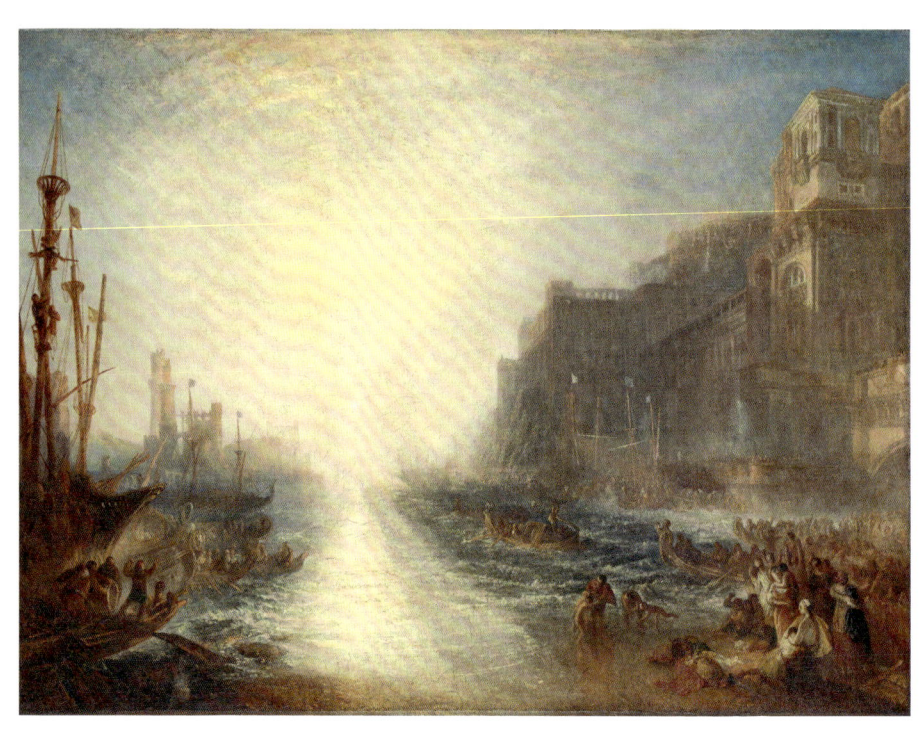

Regulus exh.1828, reworked
and exh.1837
Oil paint on canvas
89.5 × 123.8

Ulysses deriding Polyphemus –
Homer's Odyssey exh.1829
Oil paint on canvas
132.5 × 203

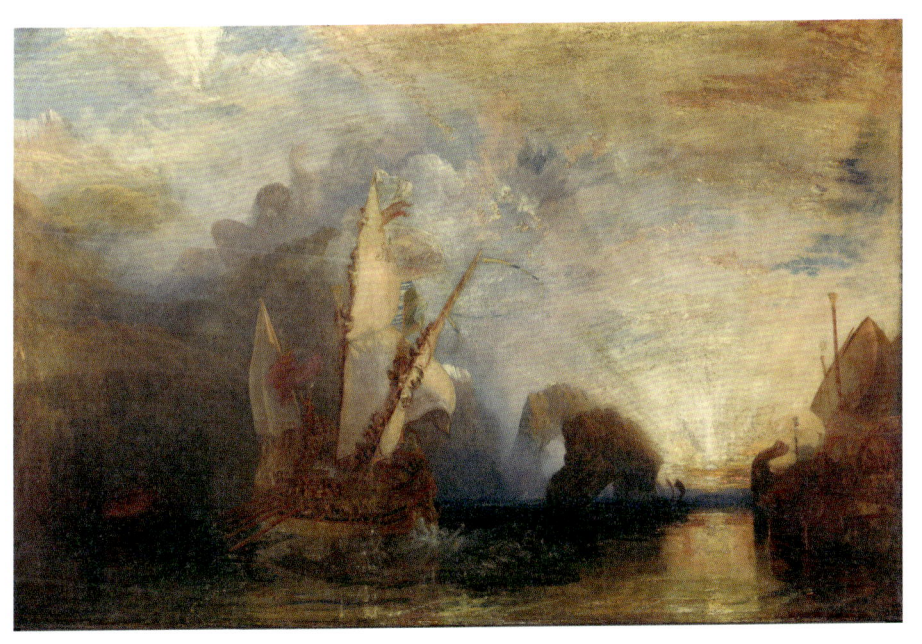

Dryburgh Abbey c.1832
Watercolour on paper
7.9 × 14.9

St. Herbert's Chapel c.1830–2
Pencil and watercolour
on paper
11 × 12.5

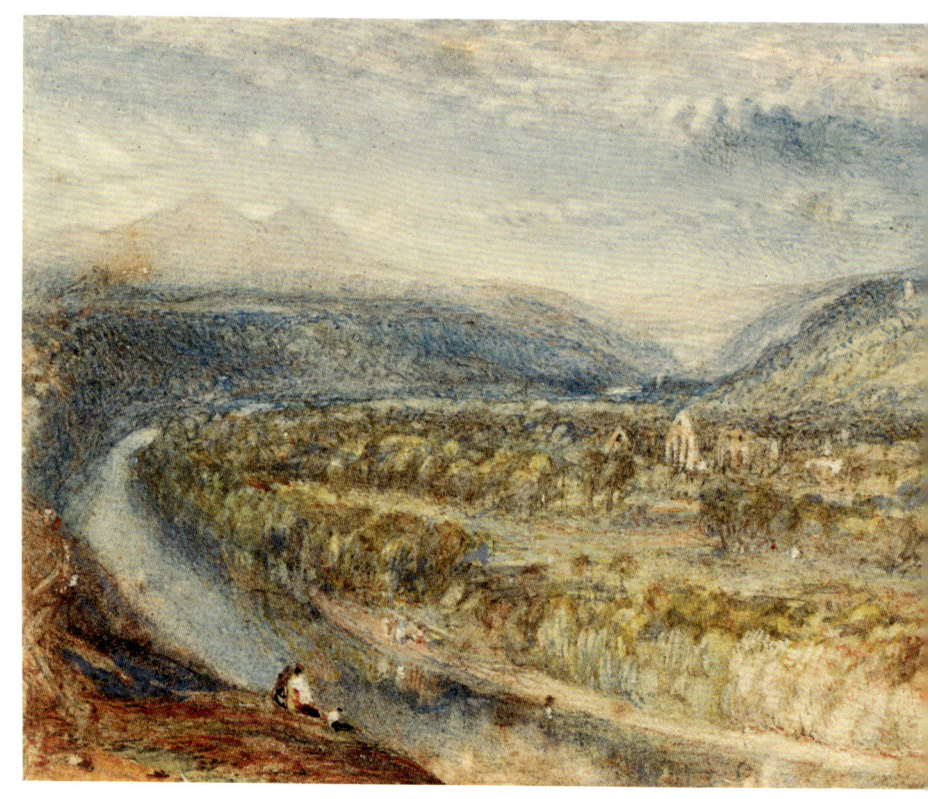

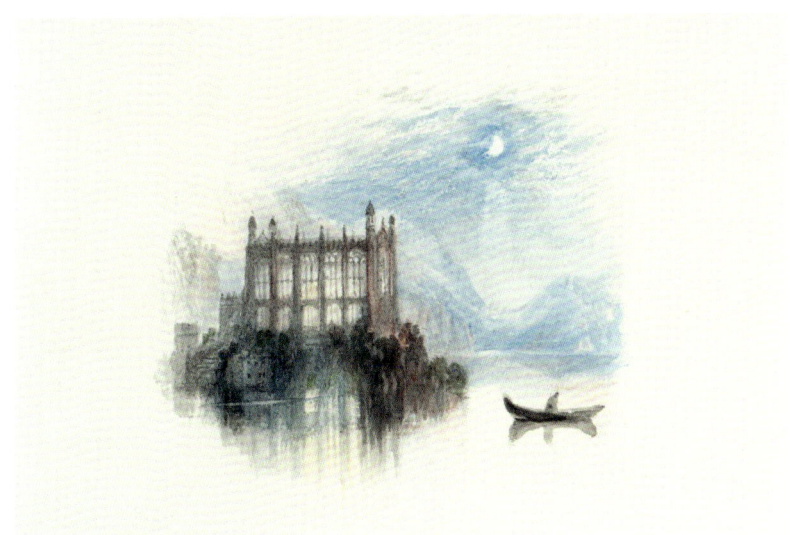

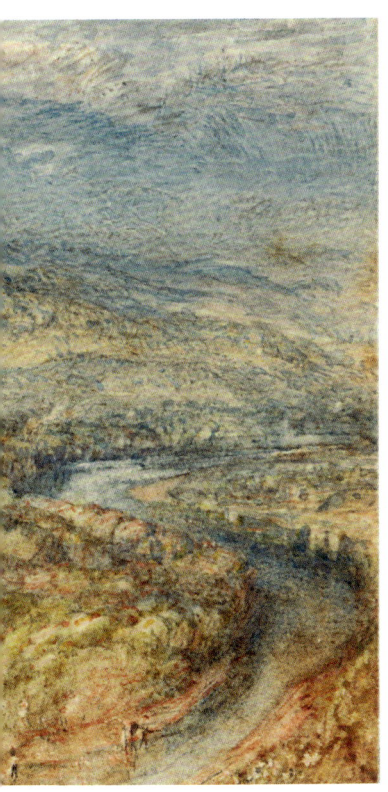

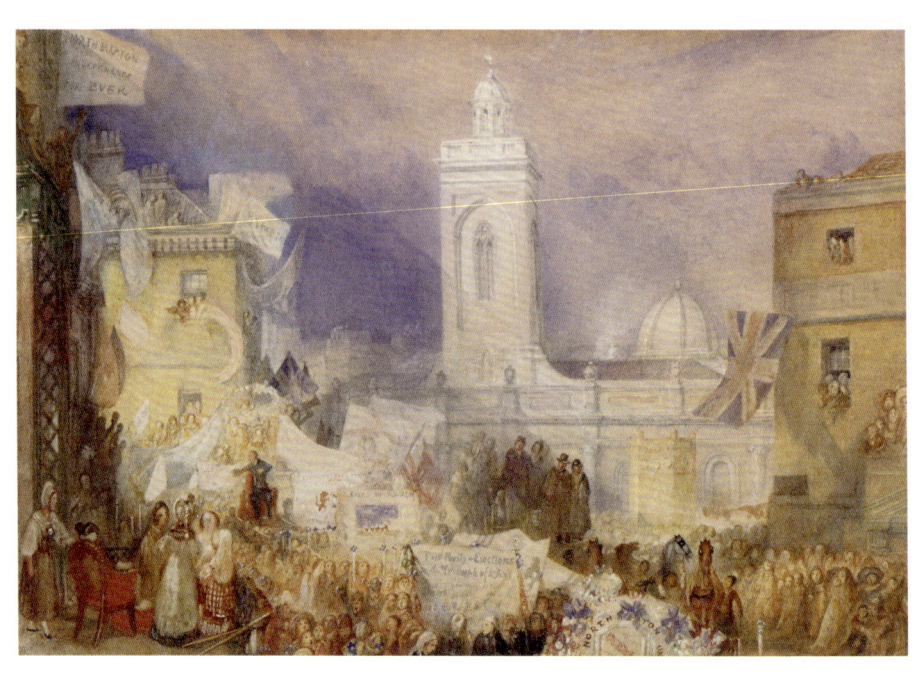

The Northampton Election,
6 December 1830 c.1830–1
Watercolour, gouache and
pen and ink on paper
29.2 × 43.8

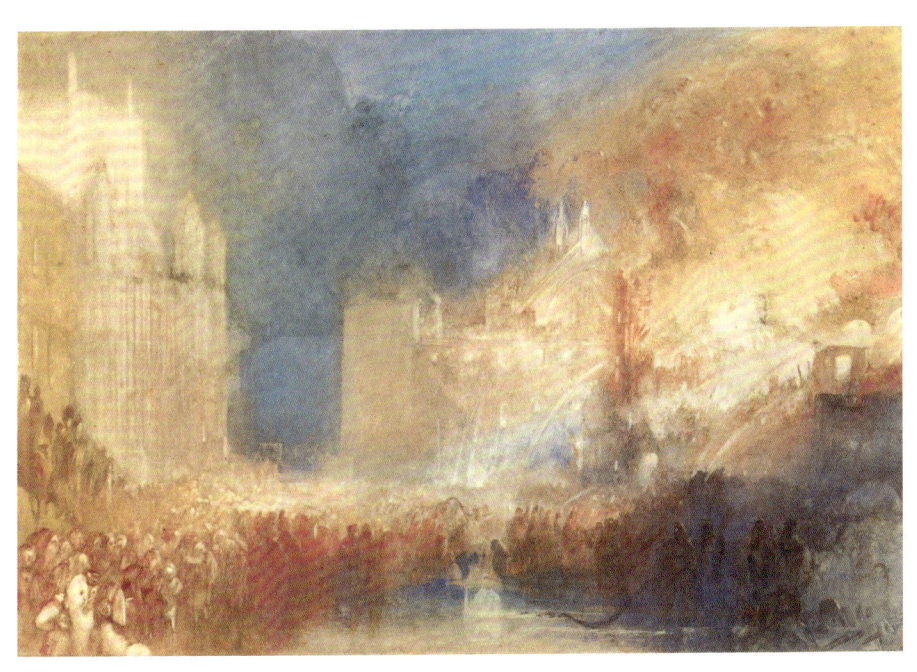

*The Burning of the Houses
of Parliament* c.1834–5
Watercolour and gouache
on paper
30.2 × 44.4

The Prince of Orange, William III, embarked from Holland, and landed at Torbay, November 4th, 1688, after a Stormy Passage exh.1832
Oil paint on canvas
90.2 × 120

A Disaster at Sea c.1835
Oil paint on canvas
171.4 × 220.3

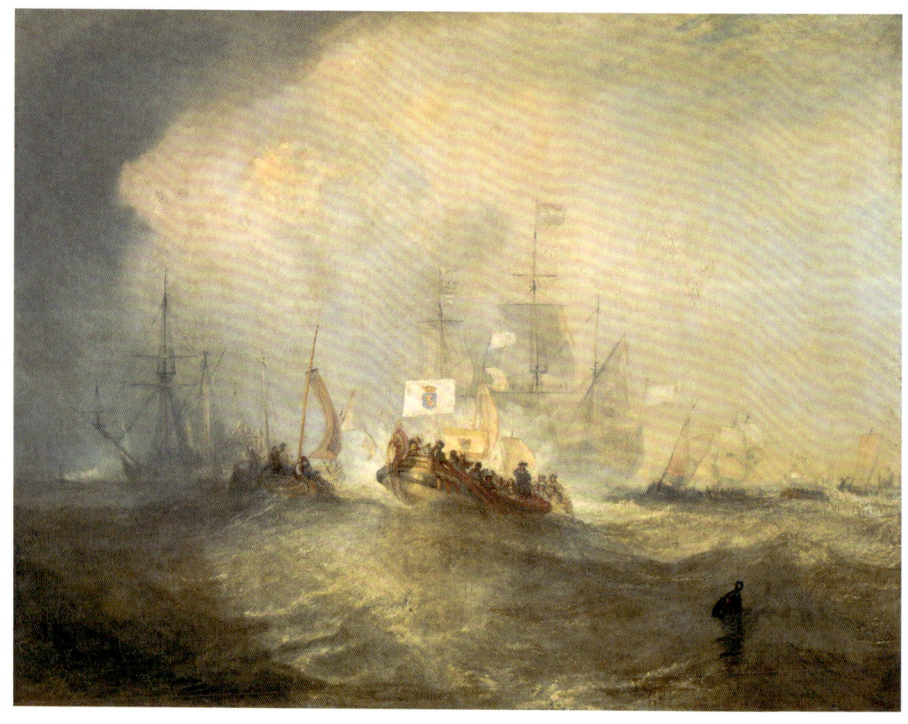

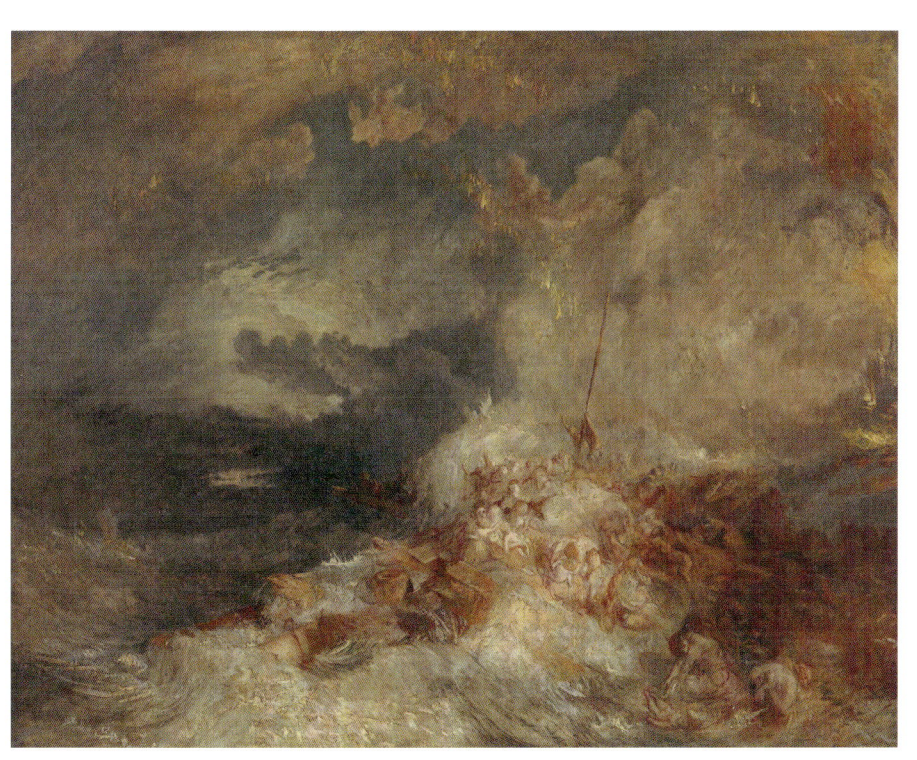

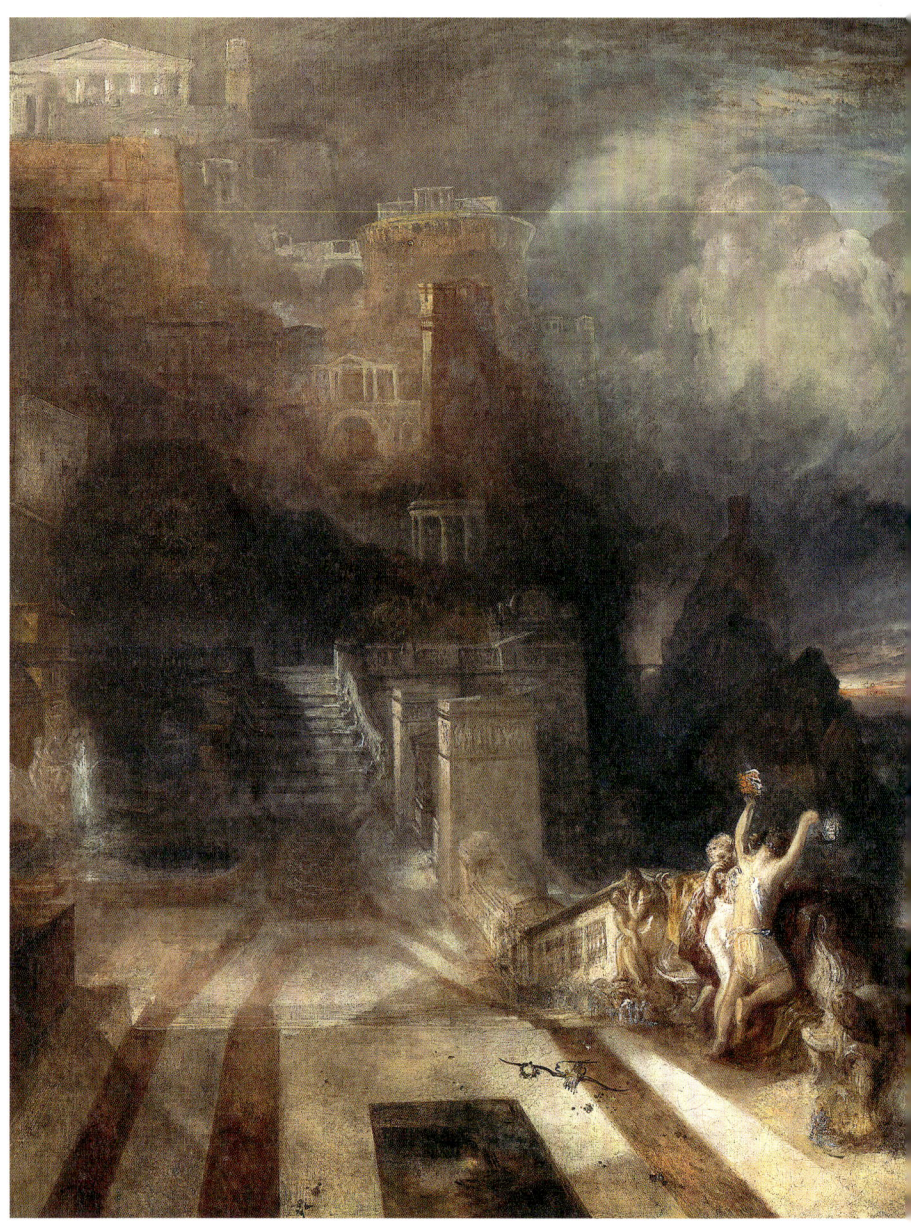

*The Parting of Hero and
Leander – from the Greek
of Musaeus* exh.1837
Oil paint on canvas
146 × 236

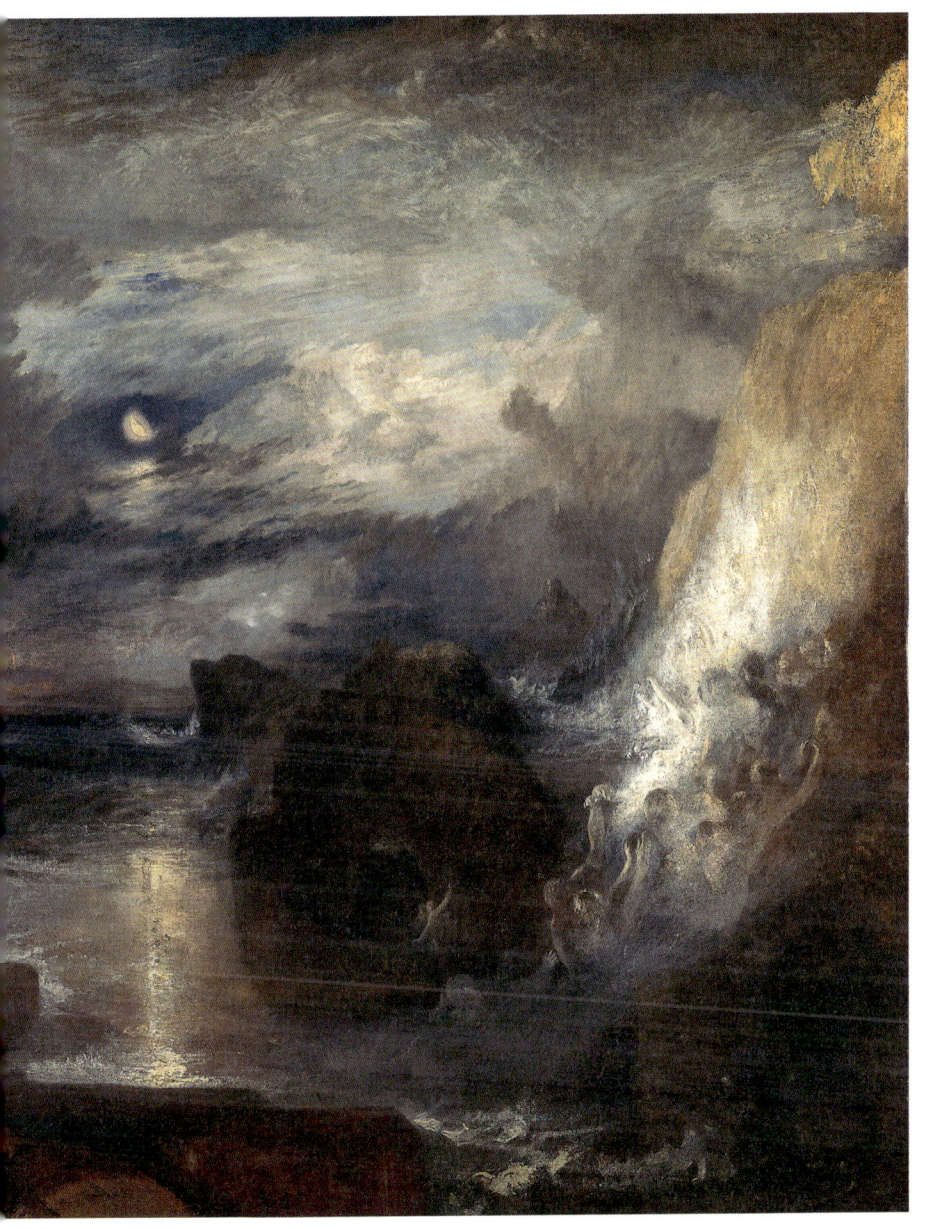

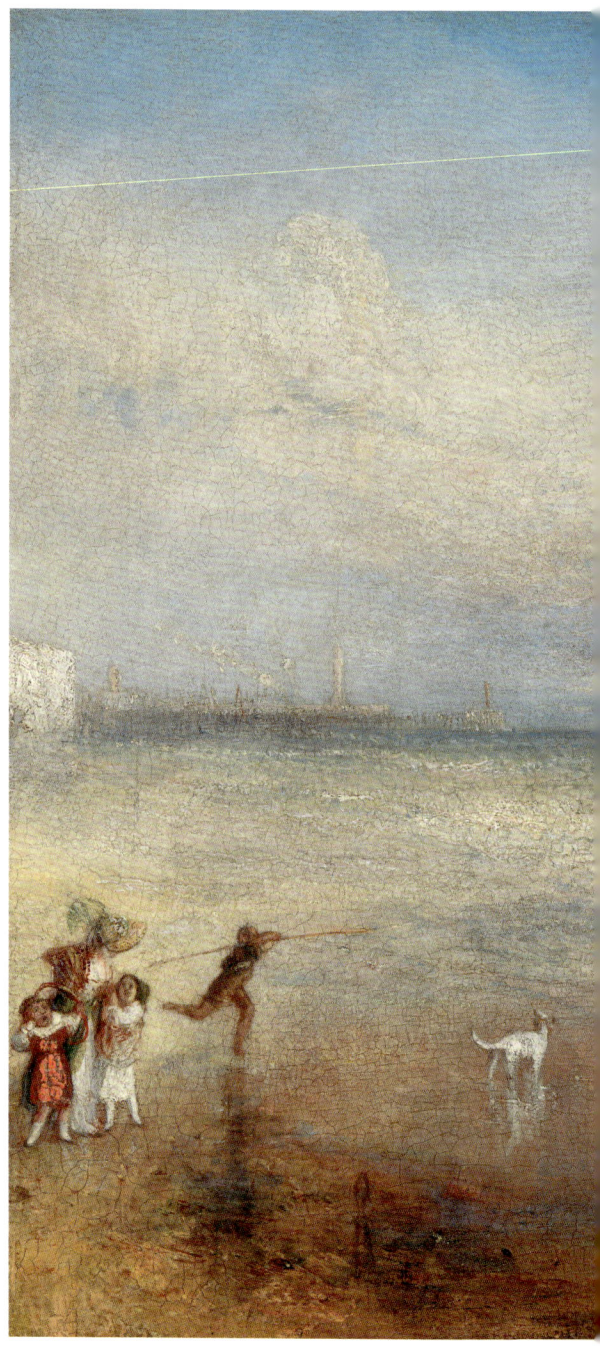

The New Moon; or 'I've lost
My Boat, You shan't have Your
Hoop' exh.1840
Oil paint on mahogany
65.4 × 81.3

OVERLEAF
The Fighting Temeraire tugged
to her last berth to be broken
up, 1838 exh.1839
Oil paint on canvas
90.7 × 121.6

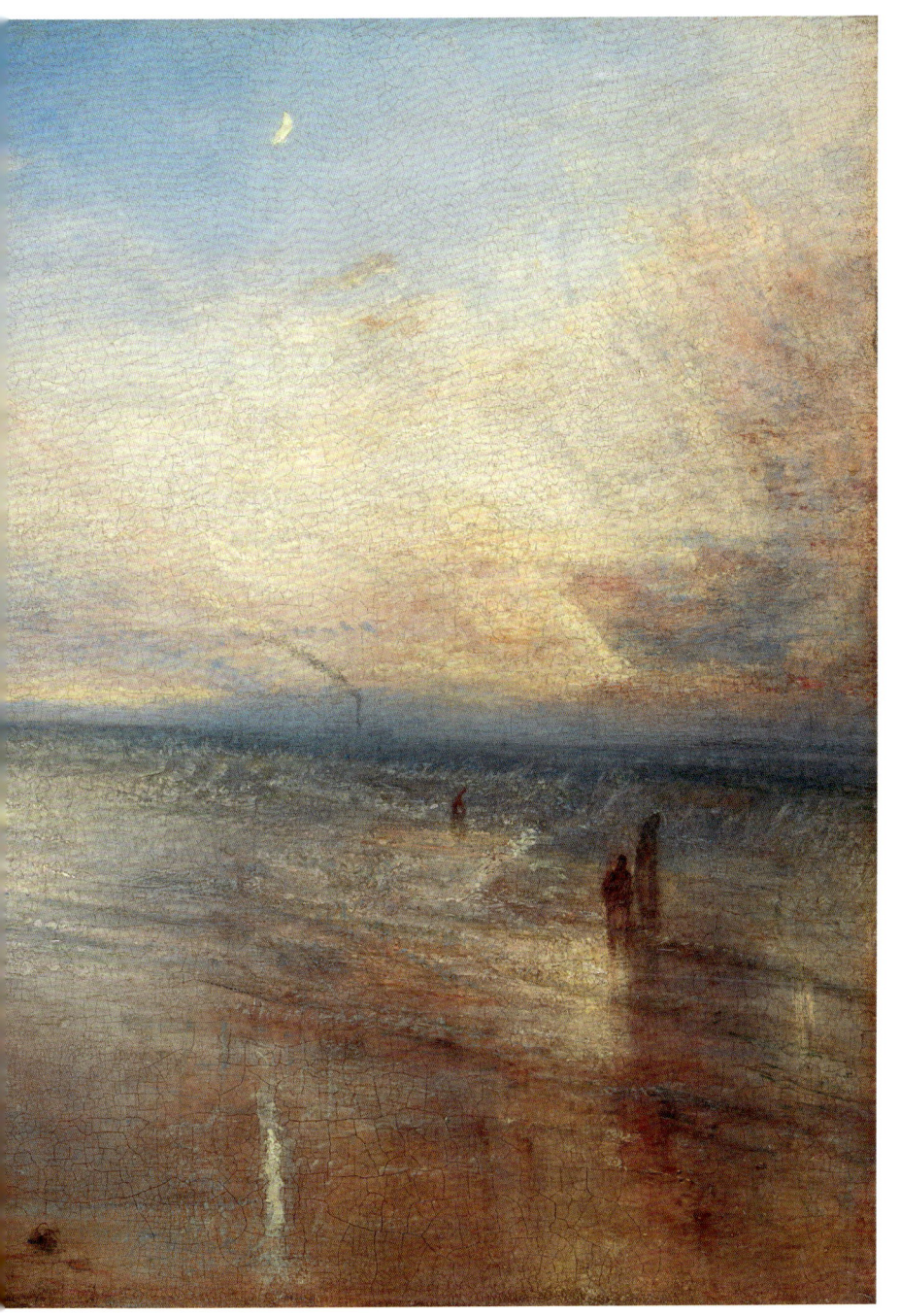

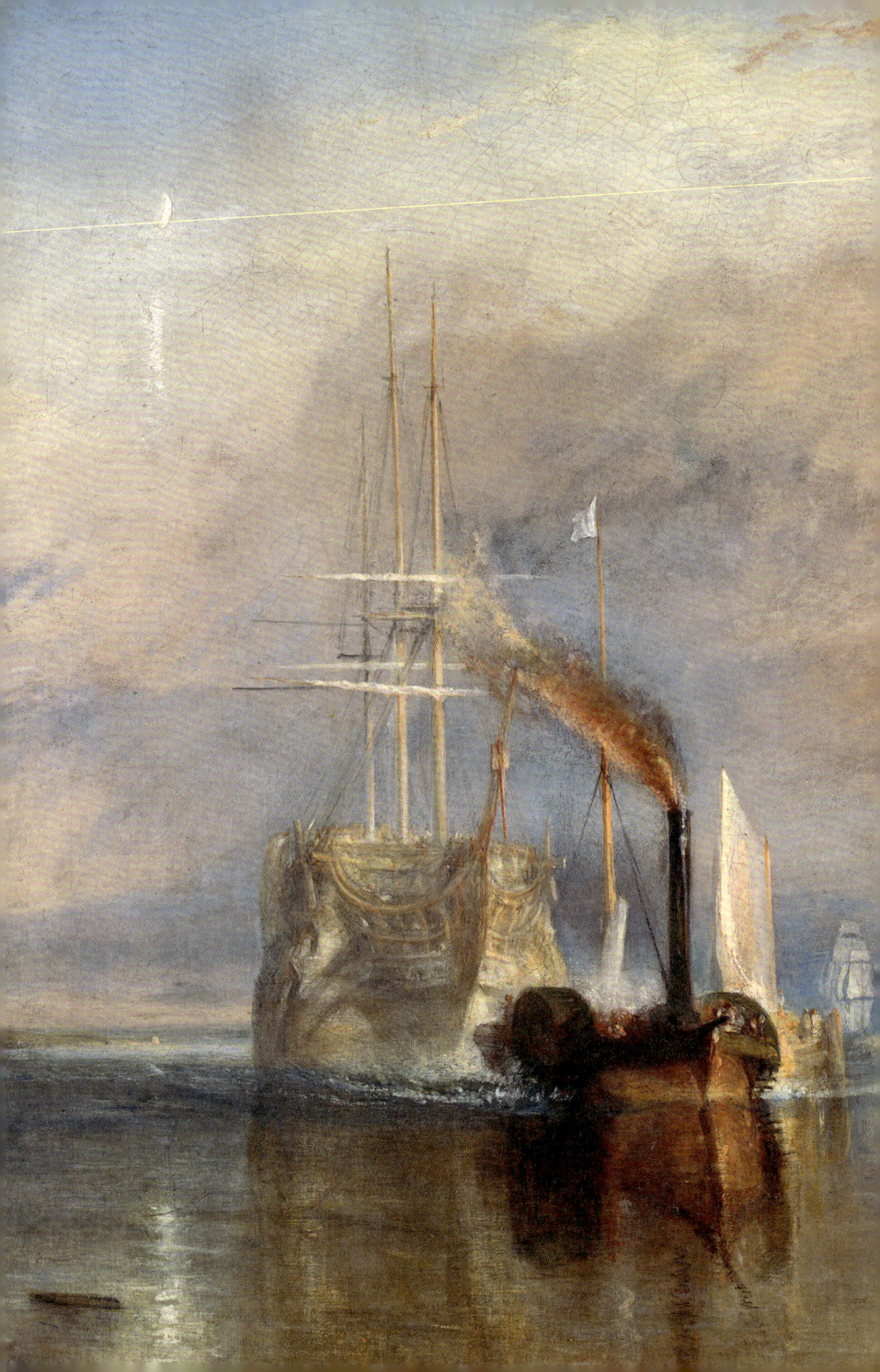

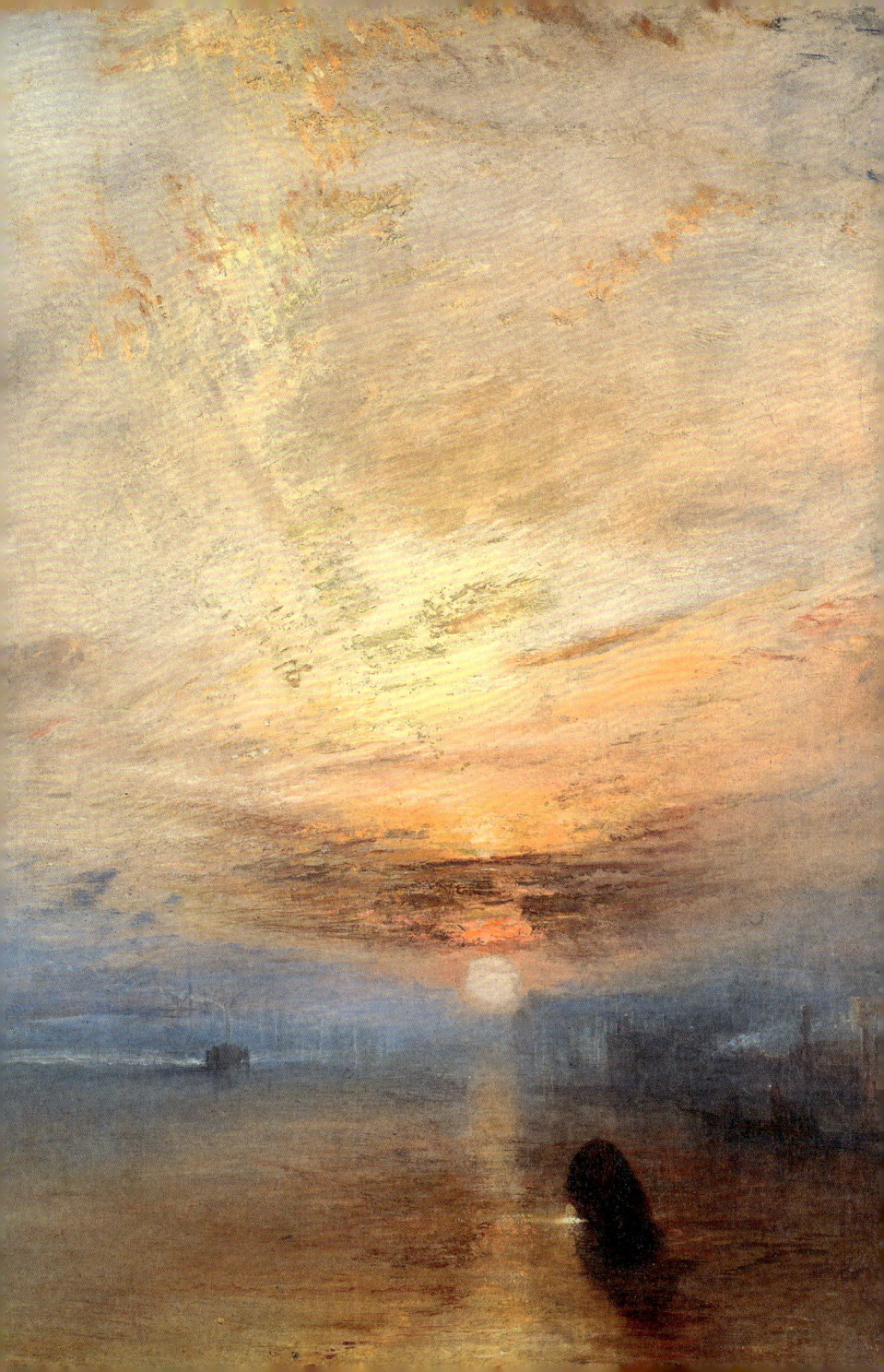

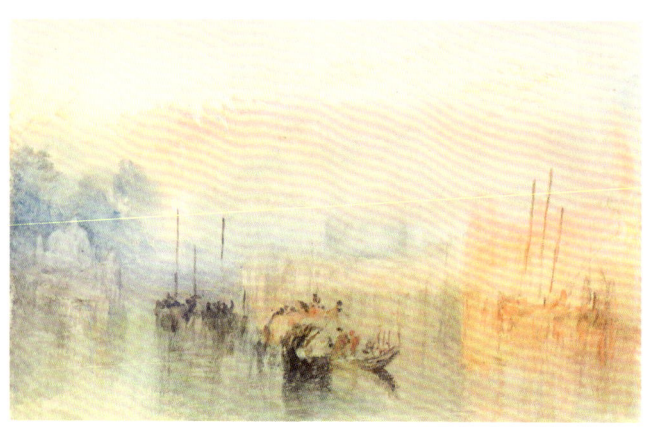

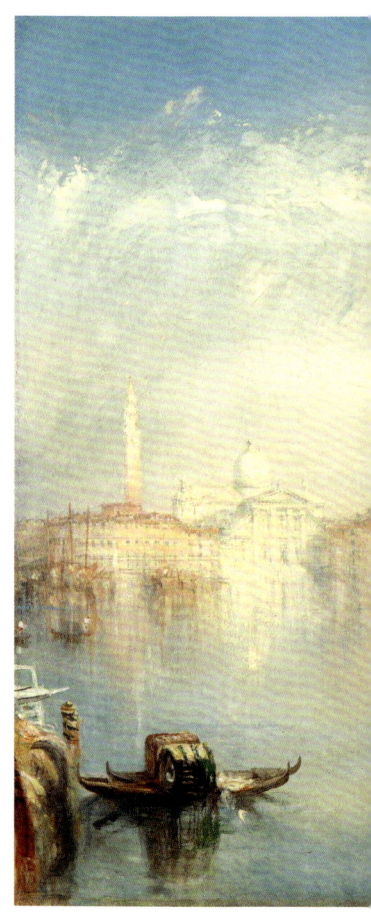

ABOVE
Shipping in the Bacino, Venice,
with Santa Maria della Salute
at the Entrance to the Grand
Canal in the Distance 1840
Watercolour on paper
22.1 × 32.1

The Dogana, San Giorgio,
Citella, from the Steps of the
Europa exh.1842
Oil paint on canvas
61.6 × 92.7

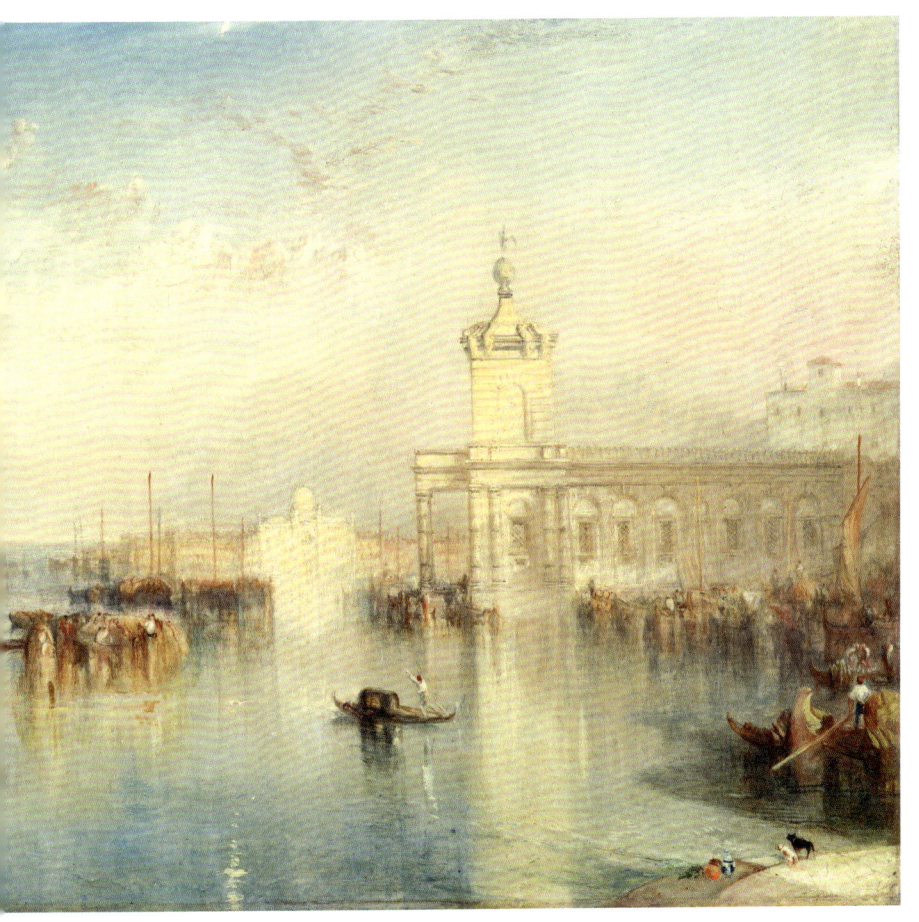

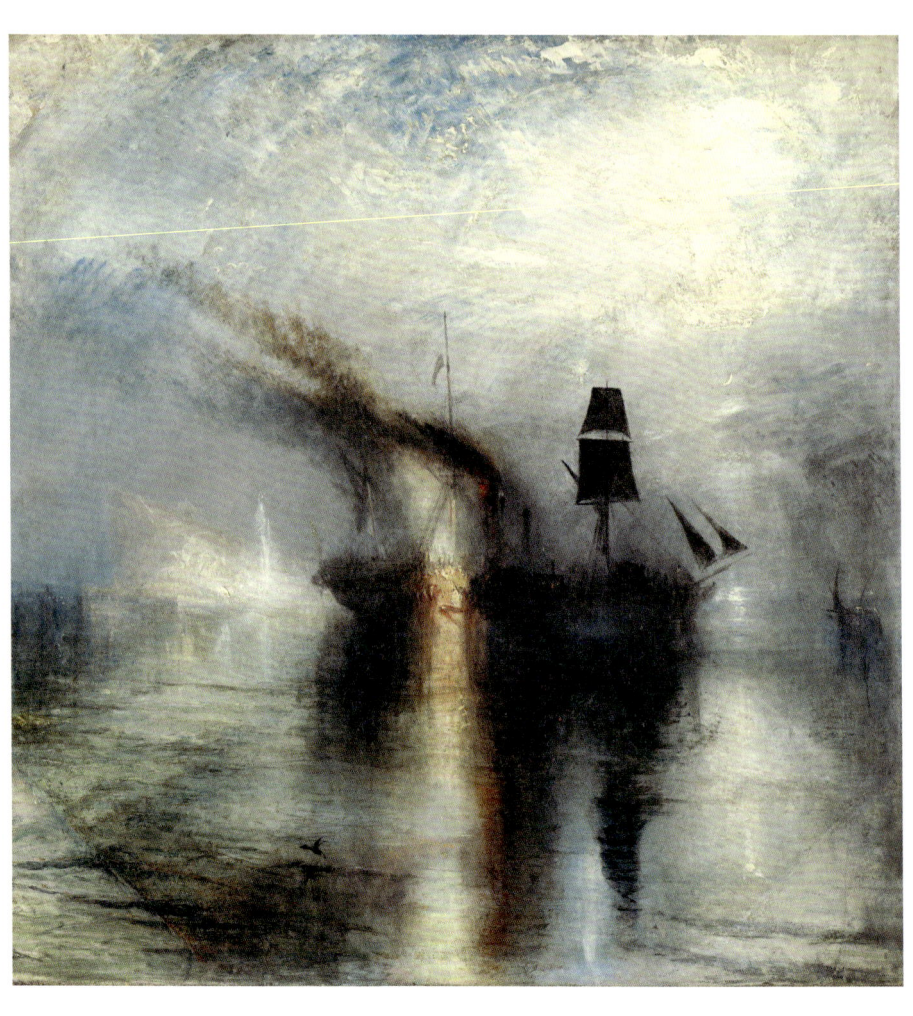

Peace – Burial at Sea exh.1842
Oil paint on canvas
87 × 86.7

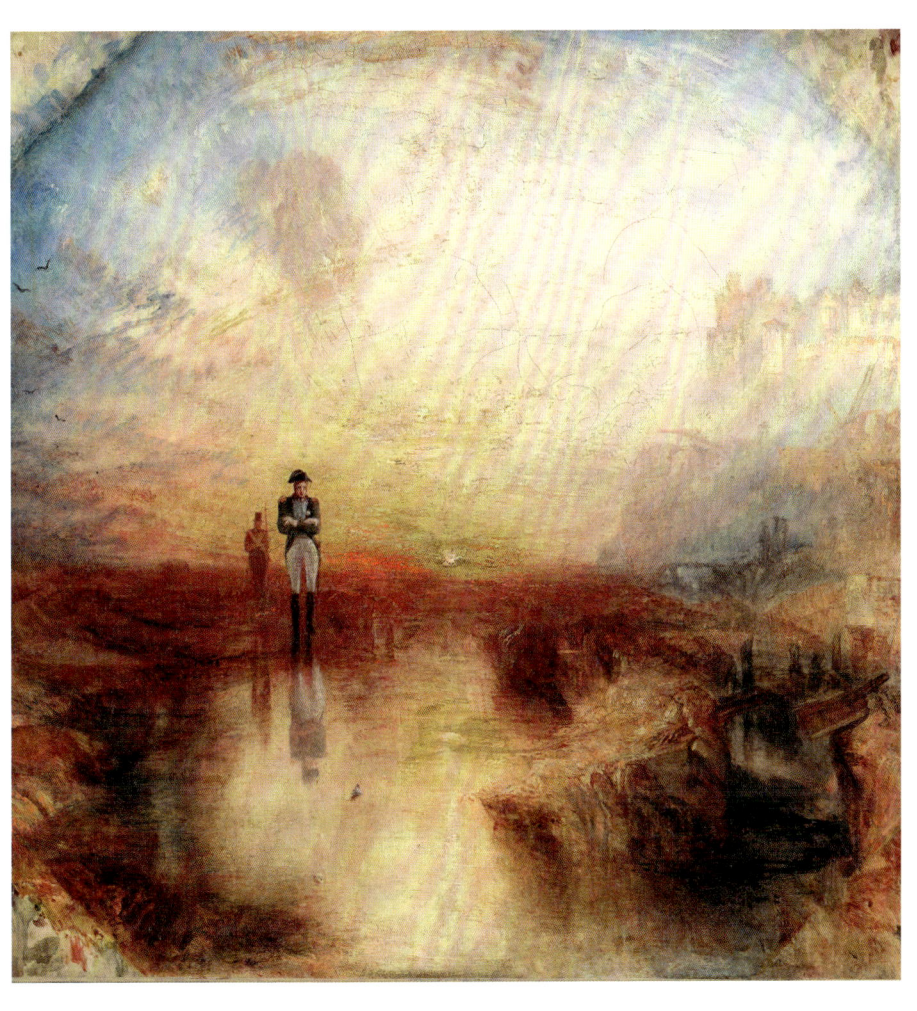

War. The Exile and the Rock
Limpet exh.1842
Turner Bequest
Oil paint on canvas
79.4 × 79.4

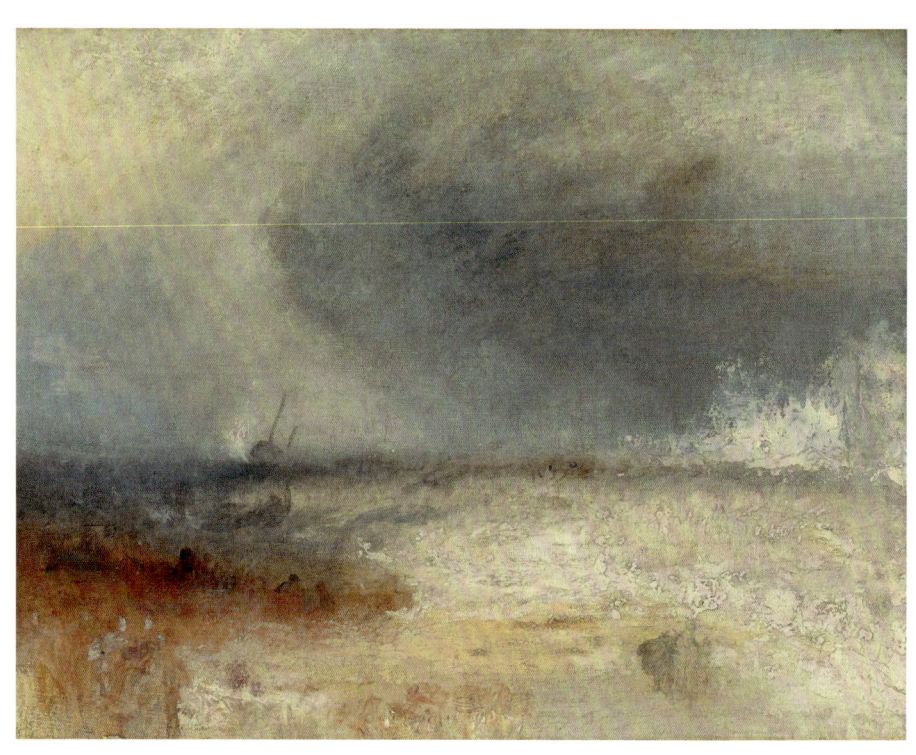

Waves Breaking on a Shore
c.1835
Oil paint on canvas
46.4 × 60.6

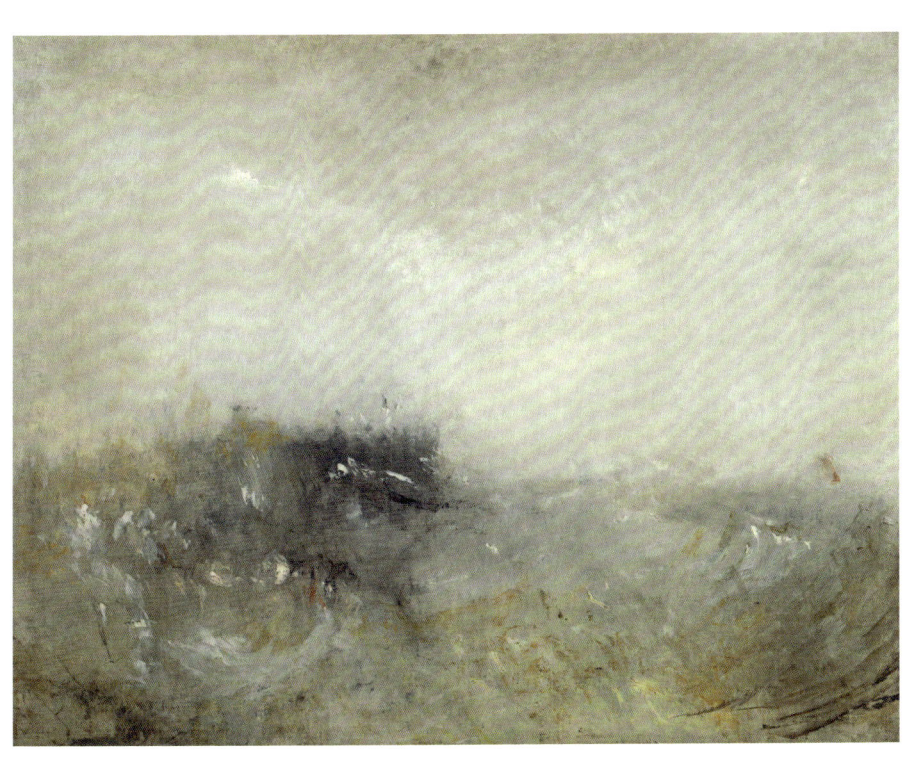

Rough Sea c.1840–5
Oil paint on canvas
91.4 × 121.9

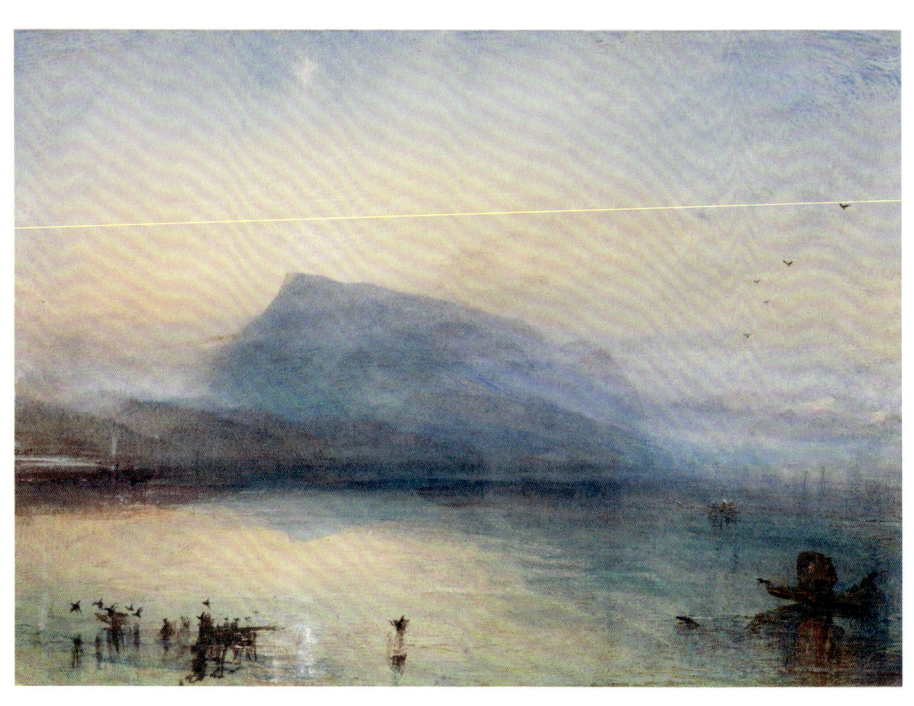

The Blue Rigi, Sunrise 1842
Watercolour on paper
29.7 × 45

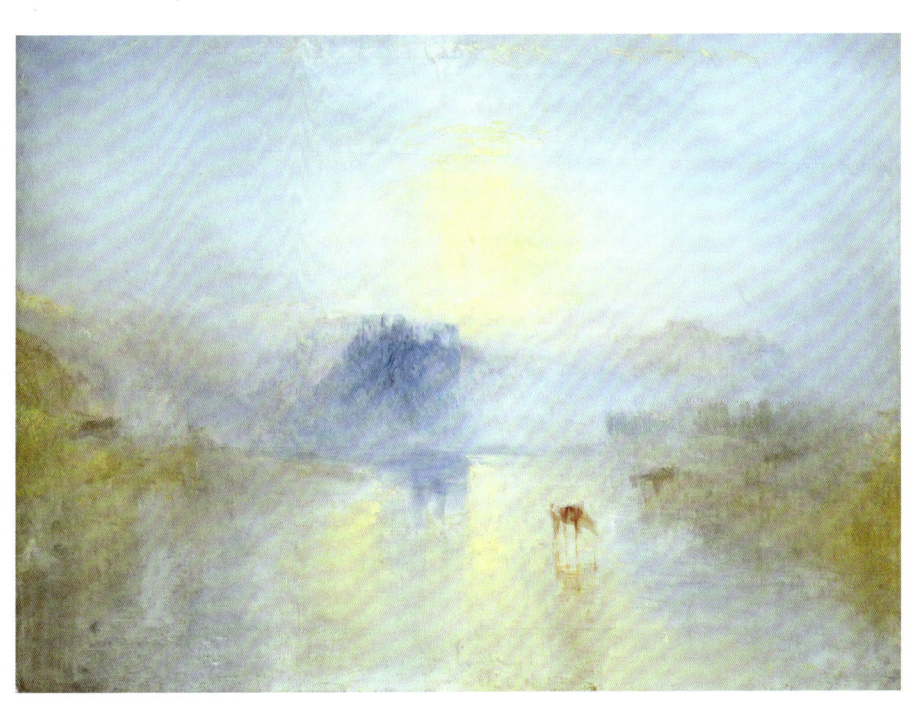

Norham Castle, Sunrise c.1845
Oil paint on canvas
90.8 × 121.9

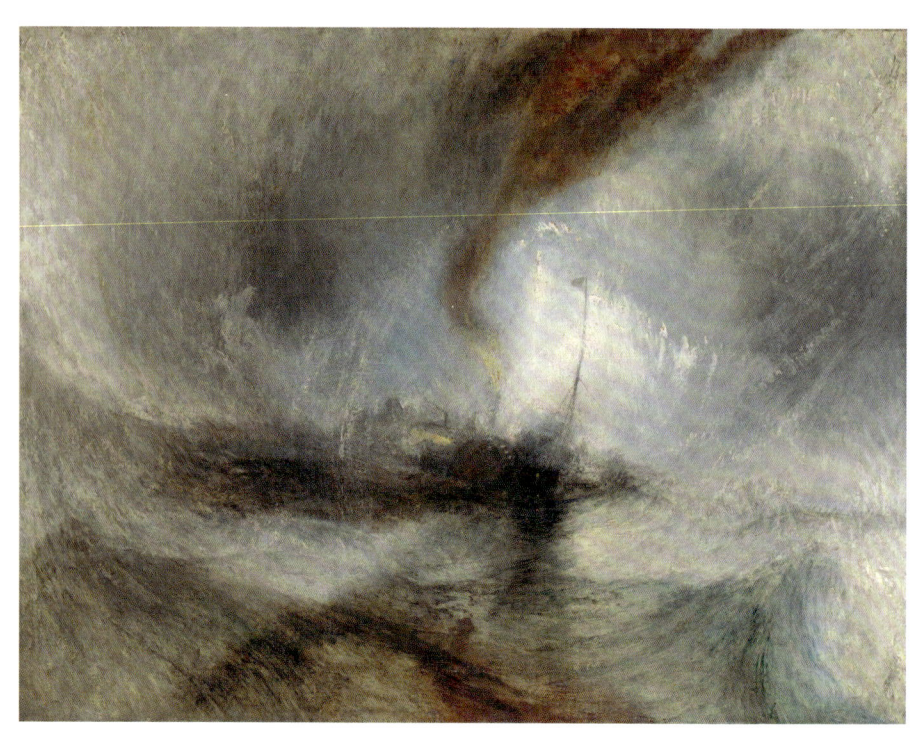

*Snowstorm – Steam-boat off
a Harbour's Mouth making
Signals in Shallow Water,
and going by the Lead. The
Author was in this Storm on
the Night the Ariel left Harwich*
exh.1842
Oil paint on canvas
91.4 × 121.9

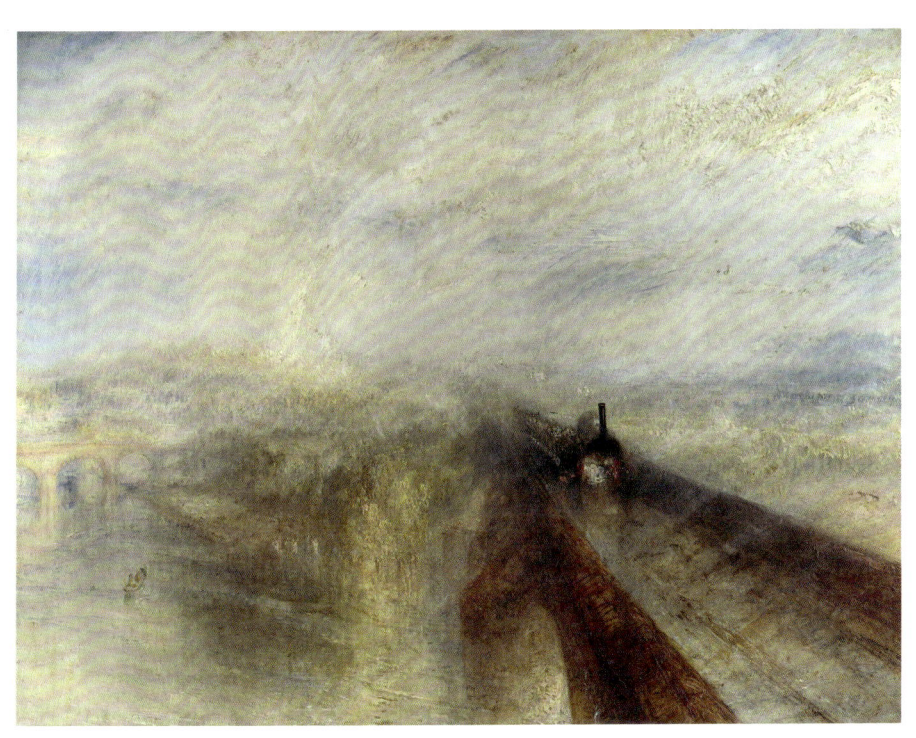

Rain, Steam, and Speed –
the Great Western Railway
exh.1844
Oil paint on canvas
91 × 121.8

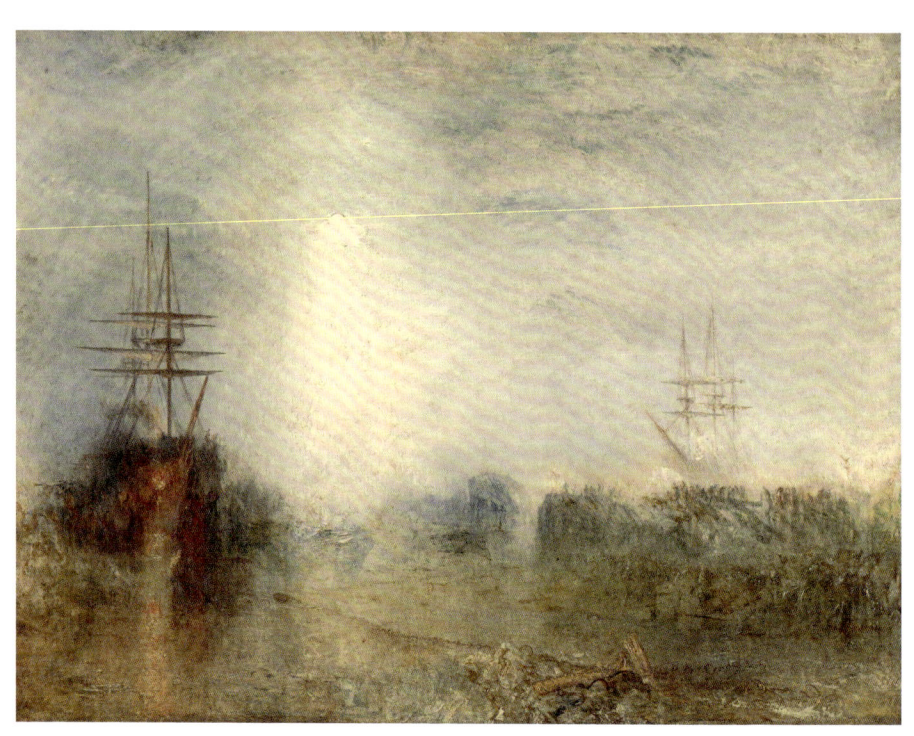

Whalers (Boiling Blubber)
Entangled in Flaw Ice,
Endeavouring to Extricate
Themselves exh.1846
Oil paint on canvas
89.9 × 120

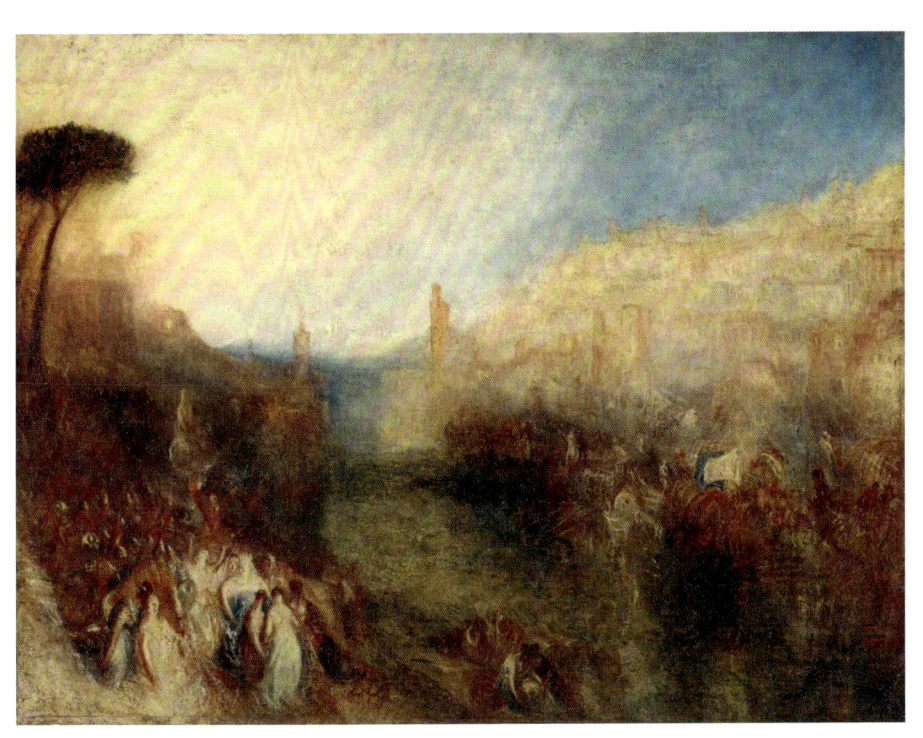

The Departure of the Fleet
exh.1850
Oil paint on canvas
89.9 × 120.3

NOTES

1. The Turner Bequest came to the nation in 1856. Turner's will stipulated that only the finished paintings in his possession (around a hundred) should form the Bequest, leaving the majority of his estate to help struggling artists. Little provision was made for Turner's relatives, who contested the will, leading to a High Court decision which allocated all his surviving works to the nation (roughly 300 oils and 30,000 drawings and watercolours) and the remaining estate to his family. The works of art originally went to the National Gallery, London, with most being transferred to the new Tate Gallery in the years after its opening in 1897. Following a flood in 1928, the works on paper were transferred to the British Museum but returned to Tate on the completion in 1987 of the Clore Gallery, built specifically to house and display the majority of the Turner Bequest (a small group of oil paintings remain at The National Gallery) alongside other works by Turner acquired separately by Tate.

2. 'What is the Turner Prize?', Tate, www.tate.org.uk/art/turner-prize, accessed 18 Jan. 2024.

3. 'About Us', Turner Contemporary, turnercontemporary.org/about, accessed 18 Jan. 2024.

4. *Rome, from Mount Aventine* exh.1836, for example, sold at Sotheby's in London in 2014 for £30.3 million, setting a new record for a work by a pre-twentieth-century British artist.

5. *Oxford English Dictionary* (2023), https://www.oed.com/search/dictionary/?scope=Entries&q=turnerian, accessed 18 Jan. 2024.

6. Several examples of Turner's well-received advice to fellow exhibitors are given by his friend and fellow artist George Jones in his memoir 'Recollections of J.M.W. Turner', reprinted in John Gage (ed.), *Collected Correspondence of J.M.W Turner*, Oxford and New York 1980, pp.1–10.

7. Turner was initially a tenant at 64 Harley Street from 1800, eventually acquiring land there to build his gallery, which opened in 1804. He subsequently acquired other adjoining land and properties, including 47 Queen Anne Street West (now demolished) which he rebuilt with a new gallery and studio to form his principal residence from 1820. He also bought land in Twickenham in 1807, building Sandycombe Lodge by 1813. He sold it in 1826 and it is now open to the public as Turner's House.

8. Letter to Maria Bicknell, 30 June 1813, published in C.R. Leslie, *Memoirs of the Life of John Constable* (1843), London 1995, p.38.

9. A volume of Henry Boswell's *Historical Descriptions of New and Elegant Picturesque Views of the Antiquities of England and Wales* (1786) owned by the distillery foreman John Lees features some seventy (out of 489) plates coloured by Turner. It is now the property of the London Borough of Hounslow Libraries.

10. Turner also received the necessary testimony of a Royal Academician from John Francis Rigaud, to whom he was introduced by the Reverend Robert Nixon; the latter had first seen Turner's drawings in the barber's shop run by the artist's father and became his firm friend.

11. *Morning Post*, 24 May 1794, quoted in Ian Warrell, '"The Wonder-Working Artist": Contemporary Responses to Turner's Exhibited and Engraved Watercolours' in *Turner: The Great Watercolours*, exh. cat., Royal Academy, London 2000, p.34.

12. John Ruskin, *Modern Painters*, vol.4, London 1856, quoted in A.J. Finberg, *Ruskin's Modern Painters*, London 1927, p.181.

13. *Studies in the Louvre* sketchbook, Tate: Turner Bequest LXXII.

14. Turner's manuscript notes for this lecture are in the British Library, and are published in John Gage, *Colour in Turner: Poetry in Truth*, London 1969, p.214, and quoted in James Hamilton, *Turner's Britain*, exh. cat., Birmingham Museum and Art Gallery, 2003, p.122.

15. Turner would have seen Rembrandt van Rijn's *Landscape with the Rest on the Flight into Egypt* 1647 (National Gallery of Ireland, Dublin) at Stourhead, Wiltshire when the work was owned by his patron there, Sir Richard Colt Hoare.

16. Turner's daughters were Evelina (b.1800/1) and Georgiana (b.1811/12). Remarks made by Turner's friends the Trimmer family have plausibly led to the identification of Evelina as a model for *Frosty Morning*

exh.1813 and *Crossing the Brook* exh.1815; see Eric Shanes, *Young Mr Turner: The First Forty Years*, New Haven 2016, p.452.

17. John Ruskin, 'Notes on the Turner Gallery at Marlborough House' (1856) in E.T. Cook and Alexander Wedderburn (eds.), *The Works of John Ruskin*, Cambridge 1904, vol.13, p.105.

18. Walter Thornbury, *The Life of J.M.W. Turner, R.A.*, London 1862, vol.1, p.8.

19. This can be seen particularly in the review by John Landseer in *The Review of Publications of Art* following Turner's re-exhibition of the painting at his own gallery in 1808. For this and other references connecting Turner's work with that of Poussin, see Martin Butlin and Evelyn Joll, *The Paintings of J.M.W. Turner*, New Haven 1984, pp.45–6.

20. Matthew Cotes Wyatt's monumental statue was installed on the Wellington Arch at Hyde Park Corner in 1846. It was moved in the 1880s to the military town of Aldershot, where it remains today.

21. Butlin and Joll 1984, p.247

22. The female convict ship the *Amphitrite* sailed from London in August 1833 and was wrecked off the French coast with the loss of over one hundred people, largely due to the captain's refusal to accept help. The *Hibernia* left Liverpool in December 1832 and caught fire in the South Atlantic with the loss of over 150 people, many of whom might have been saved had there been more lifeboats. See Sam Smiles, 'Turner's A Disaster at Sea – A New Interpretation',

Turner Society News, no.138, Autumn 2022, pp.3–7 for the suggestion of the *Hibernia* as a source and a discussion of Cecilia Powell's earlier piece on the *Amphitrite*.

23. In 1781, the crew of the *Zong* murdered 133 disease-ridden passengers bound for slavery in Jamaica. The terms of the ship's insurance meant a claim could only be made for those lost at sea. The captain, Luke Collingwood, died shortly after the incident and despite several efforts no-one was ever prosecuted.

24. One such patron was the Jamaican-plantation owner and Sussex MP John Fuller, who commissioned the *Views in Sussex* (p.16) and bought other works from Turner.

25. For a pioneering and detailed overview of the subject, see Sam Smiles, 'Turner and the Slave Trade: Speculation and representation, 1805–1840', *British Art Journal*, vol.8, no.3 (Winter 2007–8), pp.47–54.

26. The French impressionist Claude Monet, for example, described *Frosty Morning* exh.1813 (p.55) as 'painted with eyes open'. Quoted in Butlin and Joll 1984, p.91.

27. Turner's stipulation in his will that this and his *Dido Building Carthage* 1815 should be hung between Claude's 1648 works *Seaport with the Embarkation of the Queen of Sheba* and *Landscape with the Marriage of Isaac and Rebecca* at the National Gallery is still upheld today.

28. *Morning Chronicle*, 3 May 1830, quoted in Butlin and Joll 1984, p.187.

FURTHER READING

Fred G.H. Bachrach, *Turner's Holland*, exh. cat., Tate Gallery, London 1994.

Anthony Bailey, *Standing in the Sun: A Life of J.M.W. Turner*, London 1997.

David Blayney Brown (ed.), *J.M.W. Turner: Sketchbooks, Drawings and Watercolours*, Tate Research Publication, https://www.tate.org.uk/art/research-publications/jmw-turner, accessed 7 Feb 2024.

David Blayney Brown, *Turner in the Alps, 1802*, exh. cat., Tate Gallery, London 1998.

David Blayney Brown, Amy Concannon, James Finch and Sam Smiles, *Turner's Modern World*, exh. cat., Tate Britain, London 2020.

David Blayney Brown, Amy Concannon and Sam Smiles (eds.), *Late Turner: Painting Set Free*, exh. cat., Tate Britain, London 2014.

Martin Butlin and Evelyn Joll, *The Paintings of J.M.W. Turner*, revised edn., 2.vols., New Haven 1984.

Maurice Davies, *Turner as Professor: The Artist and Linear Perspective*, exh. cat., Tate Gallery, London 1992.

A.J. Finberg (ed.), *Ruskin's Modern Painters*, London 1927.

Gillian Forrester, *Turner's 'Drawing Book': The Liber Studiorum*, exh. cat., Tate Gallery, London 1996.

John Gage (ed.), *Collected Correspondence of J.M.W. Turner*, Oxford and New York 1980.

John Gage, *J.M.W. Turner: 'A Wonderful Range of Mind'*, New Haven 1987.

James Hamilton, *Turner: A Life*, London 1997.

James Hamilton, *Turner's Britain*, exh. cat., Birmingham Museums and Art Gallery, Birmingham 2003.

James Hamilton, *Turner: The Late Seascapes*, exh. cat., Sterling and Francine Clark Art Institute, New Haven 2003.

David Hill, *Turner on the Thames: River Journeys in the Year 1805*, New Haven 1993.

Evelyn Joll, Martin Butlin and Luke Herrmann (eds.), *The Oxford Companion to J.M.W. Turner*, Oxford 2001.

Anne Lyles and Diane Perkins, *Colour into Line: Turner and the Art of Engraving*, exh. cat., Tate Gallery, London 1989.

Franny Moyle, *The Extraordinary Life and Momentous Times of J.M.W. Turner*, London 2016.

Jan Piggott, *Turner's Vignettes*, exh. cat., Tate Gallery, London 1989.

Cecilia Power, *Turner's Rivers of Europe: The Rhine, Meuse, and Mosel*, exh. cat., Tate Gallery, London 1991.

Christine Riding and Richard Johns (eds.), *Turner and the Sea*, exh. cat., National Maritime Museum, London 2013.

Christopher Rowell, Ian Warrell and David Blayney Brown, *Turner at Petworth*, exh. cat., Petworth House, West Sussex 2002.

Eric Shanes, *Turner's England, 1810–38*, London 1990.

Eric Shanes, *Young Mr Turner – The First Forty Years*, 1775–1815, New Haven 2016.

Sam Smiles, *The Turner Book*, London 2006.

David Solkin (ed.), *Turner and the Masters*, exh. cat., Tate Britain, London 2009.

Joyce Townsend, *Turner's Painting Techniques*, exh. cat., Tate Gallery, London 1993.

Ian Warrell (ed.), *J.M.W. Turner*, exh. cat., National Gallery of Art, Washington/Dallas Museum of Art/Metropolitan Museum of Art, New York 2007.

Ian Warrell, *Through Switzerland with Turner: Ruskin's First Selection from the Turner Bequest*, exh. cat., Tate Gallery, London 1995.

Ian Warrell et al., *Turner and Venice*, exh. cat., Tate Britain, London 2003.

Ian Warrell, *Turner on the Loire*, exh. cat., Tate Gallery, London 1997.

Ian Warrell, *Turner on the Seine*, exh. cat., Tate Gallery, London 1999.

Andrew Wilton, *The Life and Work of J.M.W. Turner*, London and Fribourg 1979.

Andrew Wilton, *Turner in his Time*, London 1987.

INDEX

Page references in italics indicate images.

CREDITS

First published 2024 by order of the Tate Trustees
by Tate Publishing, a division of Tate Enterprises Ltd
Millbank, London SW1P 4RG
www.tate.org.uk/publishing

A catalogue record for this book is available from
the British Library

ISBN 978 1 84976 903 7

Distributed in the United States and Canada
by ABRAMS, New York
Library of Congress Control Number applied for

Senior Editor: Emma Poulter
Production: Bill Jones
Picture Researcher: Emma O'Neill
Designed by Astrid Stavro
Colour reproduction by DL Imaging, London Printed
and bound in Italy by Printer Trento S.r.l

Cover: *Waves Breaking on a Shore* c.1835
(detail, see p.84)

Frontispiece: *Snowstorm – Steam-boat off a Harbour's
Mouth*... exh.1842 (detail, see p.88)

Measurements of artworks are given in centimetres,
height before width and depth

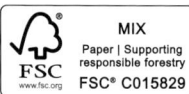

ABOUT THE AUTHOR
Andrew Loukes is Curator of the Egremont Collection
at Petworth House, having previously worked at Tate
Britain and Manchester Art Gallery. He is a specialist
in British art of the Romantic period and has curated
several exhibitions on J.M.W. Turner, along with
others on John Constable and William Blake. Andrew
is also a former Trustee of Turner's House.